THE ABINGDON WORSHIP ANNUAL

2007

CONTEMPORARY & TRADITIONAL
RESOURCES FOR WORSHIP LEADERS

The

ABINGDON

WORSHIP

Annual

2007

EDITED BY MARY J. SCIFRES & B. J. BEU

Abingdon Press
Nashville

THE ABINGDON WORSHIP ANNUAL 2007
CONTEMPORARY AND TRADITIONAL RESOURCES FOR WORSHIP LEADERS

Copyright © 2006 by Abingdon Press

This book is printed on acid-free paper.

ISBN 0-687-49755-8
ISBN-13: 978-0-687-49755-3

06 07 08 09 10 11 12 13 14 15—10 9 8 7 6 5 4 3 2

MANUFACTURED IN THE UNITED STATES OF AMERICA

CONTENTS

MAY

JUNE

JULY

AUGUST

SEPTEMBER

OCTOBER

NOVEMBER

DECEMBER

INTRODUCTION

"Plan or perish!" This could be the motto of worship leadership across Christianity's wide spectrum. Worship that is thrown together or is simply a conglomeration of pieces plopped into place, is seldom satisfying to anyone. But well-planned worship is an accomplishment of great satisfaction to the planners, as well as an entry point of great possibility for worshipers. Only the Holy Spirit has the power to transform our plans into miraculous encounters with God, but careful planning on our part allows the Spirit to move fluidly through a service, touching different people in different ways, and allowing people from a diversity of backgrounds to experience the holiness of God.

Into this process of planning, we offer the following pages. Knowing that you are undoubtedly busy with other pastoral duties, rehearsal obligations, or ministry needs, we have designed this resource to lift some of the burdensome nature of worship planning, while enhancing your creativity in molding a worship service together. As you review the suggestions contained herein, feel free to rework, lengthen, or shorten prayers and litanies. If an image we provide sparks an urge to write your own prayer, run with it! If you find yourself choosing to use a different scripture than the day's lections, thumb to the Scripture Index of this year's or previous *Worship Annuals* to find the right resource.

The Abingdon Worship Annual offers liturgical resources for both traditional and contemporary worship. For each Sunday of the year (and most holy days), we provide resources to help plan your corporate worship services.

Each entry includes: Calls to Worship, Opening Prayers, Praise Sentences, Contemporary Gathering Words, Prayers of Confession or Unison Prayers, and Benedictions. The Praise Sentences and Contemporary Gathering Words fit the spontaneous and informal nature of many nontraditional worship styles. These are particularly helpful to those leading contemporary worship. The Calls to Worship, Unison Prayers, and Benedictions are more traditional in style. But many of these entries are adaptable for any style of worship. In all cases, the readings are scripture-referenced and lectionary-based.

You may notice that *The Abingdon Worship Annual* was written to complement *The Abingdon Preaching Annual*. But *The Abingdon Worship Annual* is also well suited to complement *Prepare! A Weekly Worship Planbook for Pastors and Musicians* or *The United Methodist Music and Worship Planner*. Together, this trinity of resources provides the music, the words, and the preaching guidance to plan integrated and coordinated worship services. Well-coordinated services do not happen in a vacuum; they require careful planning—planning that congregation members recognize and appreciate. These resources facilitate such planning on a weekly basis.

All contributions in *The Abingdon Worship Annual* are based upon readings from *The Revised Common Lectionary*. As you plan worship, we encourage you to begin with Scripture in mind. Read the lections aloud and note those words that speak "prayer" or "song" or "image" to you. Reflect thoughtfully and prayerfully. Then, read through the many ideas inspired by those scriptures. Read these ideas aloud as well, listening for the prayers that speak to you or the litanies that will inspire your congregation. A single line may inspire a song or hymn selection, or a theme may jump out and say "preach this!" Let this resource be a creative trampoline, lifting you into joyous thinking and reflection as you plan worship to its fullest.

The words before you will vary in style and content, as do their contributors, who come from a wide variety of theological and denominational backgrounds. We hope you like the diversity as much as we do!

As you work with the 2007 edition of *The Abingdon Worship Annual*, some explanations may be helpful in using it to the fullest. Calls to Worship are words that gather God's people together as they prepare to worship. These words of greeting or gathering are typically read responsively. Some of the Contemporary Gathering Words listed in each resource may also be helpful as Calls to Worship in traditional or blended-worship settings.

As with all responsive readings, think creatively as you plan your services. While it is simplest to have a single leader read the words in light print and have the congregation respond by reading the words in bold print, it is often effective to have several people, or even groups of people, lead these calls. Using the choir, a youth group, or a small prayer group adds variety and vitality to your services. Some congregations enjoy responding to one another: women to men, right side to left side, children to parents. Experiment with a variety of options, and see how these words might be most meaningful in calling your congregation together to worship the Holy One.

Like more formal Calls to Worship, Contemporary Gathering Words are often read responsively. Unlike more formal Calls to Worship, however, Contemporary Gathering Words tend to use simpler language and are often more repetitive in nature. You may copy any and all entries onto an overhead transparency or presentation slide to help your congregation read responsively without being tied to a bulletin. The electronic version of this resource can be particularly helpful if you use presentation software or word processing for worship planning purposes.

While one leader might easily speak many of the Praise Sentences provided in this resource, the "call and response" format is an attractive option. In praise settings, worshipers are often willing to respond back in echo form, repeating the words or phrases spoken by the worship leader. Echoing the same words and phrases several times can be highly effective. The Praise Sentences in this resource are intended not to limit you, but rather to free you to lead in a more informal and free-flowing style, where appropriate.

If your congregation does not care to read words aloud, consider using two leaders to speak in call and response format. Or, allow the song team or band members to act as responders to the worship leader, echoing the call and response tradition of African American worship.

Opening Prayers are most often provided to invoke God's presence in worship and to focus worshipers on the scripture or theme for the day. Some are more informal than others, and some are more general than formal invocations. Opening prayers may be read by a single worship leader or by the whole congregation in unison. Many can be adapted for later use in the worship service, if that suits your needs.

Prayers take many forms in this resource. Some are offered as Prayers of Confession. Confessional prayers and their corresponding Words of Assurance follow many different formats. At times, the Assurance of Pardon is contained in the prayer. When it is not, we have tried to provide Words of Assurance. Favorite scriptures of comfort also provide wonderful Words of Assurance. Some prayers are in the form of a Collect and may even be adapted as Opening or Closing Prayers. Any prayer may be revised into call and response format. In all cases, we have sought to provide words that can easily be spoken by a large congregation in unison. For the sake of consistency, such entries have been given the title Unison Prayer. You may use any title you deem appropriate in your worship bulletins.

Benedictions, sometimes known as Blessings or Words of Dismissal, are included in each entry. Some work best in call and response format; others seem more appropriate as a solitary blessing from the worship leader. Choose the format best suited to your congregation. Many litanies, prayers, and calls to worship in *The Abingdon Worship Annual 2007* intersperse direct quotations from scripture with lines of text for other sources. In order to focus on the poetic nature of worship words and to facilitate the ease of use with this resource, we do not indicate these direct quotations with quotation marks.

Enjoy this resource, and enjoy the year ahead. We wish you God's blessings as you seek to share Christ's word and offer experiences of the Holy Spirit in your work and worship!

Mary J. Scifres and B. J. Beu, Editors

JANUARY 1, 2007

Watch Night/New Year
B. J. Beu

COLOR
White

SCRIPTURE READINGS
Ecclesiastes 3:1-13; Psalm 8; Revelation 21:1-6*a*; Matthew 25:31-46

THEME IDEAS
As the old year ends and the new year begins, we are faced with old realities and new possibilities. In Ecclesiastes, God reminds us that weeping, tearing down, and lying fallow are all part of the seasons and rhythms of life. If we truly want to change our lives, Scripture gives us a place to start: feeding the hungry, clothing the naked, visiting the sick and imprisoned, and comforting those who mourn. As we look with anticipation to the new year, we place our trust in the One whose glory is beheld in the new heaven and new earth—the One who will wipe away every tear.

CALL TO WORSHIP (ECCLESIASTES 3)
As we journey through life,
God is always with us.
In seasons of rejoicing,
we do not laugh alone.

1

In seasons of mourning,
we do not weep alone.
When we sow and when we reap,
we are not alone.
Come and worship God,
who holds our past, present, and future.

CALL TO WORSHIP (PSALM 8)

O God, you are wonderful.
How majestic is your name!
We behold your glory in the heavens!
**We sense your splendor
in the earth beneath our feet.**
Who are we that you are mindful of us?
Who are mortals that you care for us?
Yet you create us in your image.
We behold your glory in one another.
You entreat us to care for your creatures.
**We behold your glory
in the works of your hands.**
O God, you are wonderful!
How majestic is your name!

CALL TO WORSHIP (MATTHEW 25)

Christ is the Good Shepherd.
In Christ's love we dwell secure.
The Shepherd watches over us.
In Christ's love we dwell secure.
The Shepherd offers us the gift of eternal life.
In Christ's love we dwell secure.

CONTEMPORARY GATHERING WORDS (ECCLESIASTES 3)

God brings us to a new year.
Rejoice and be glad!
God brings us to new seasons of joy and hope.

Rejoice and be glad!
God shares our pain in seasons of sadness and loss.
Rejoice and be glad!
God brings us newness of life.
Rejoice and be glad!

PRAISE SENTENCES (PSALM 8)

God's name is above all names.
Praise God's holy name!
The works of God are a wonder to behold.
Praise God's holy name!
God's glory fills us with hope.
Praise God's holy name!

OPENING PRAYER (REVELATION 21)

Eternal God,
    foundation of heaven and earth,
        bring us into your courts,
        and usher us into the age to come.
Dwell among your people,
    and wipe away the tears from our eyes.
May our lives reflect
    the wonder of your Spirit within us,
    that others may lift their eyes
        and behold your glory.
In the name of the One
    who is the Alpha and the Omega,
    the first and the last, we pray. Amen.

OPENING PRAYER (NEW YEAR)

Eternal God,
    foundation of all that is,
    and was, and is to be,
        bless us as we come to a new year.
Help us forgive ourselves
    for our past failings.

Open our eyes,
    that we may see the possibilities
        that lie before us.
Guide our footsteps,
    that we may carry your presence
    to all those we meet. Amen.

BENEDICTION (ECCLESIASTES 3)
Rejoice in God's blessings!
God never leaves us.
Rejoice in God's blessings!
God lifts us up in times of trial.
Rejoice in God's blessings!
God is there, every step of the way.

JANUARY 7, 2007

Baptism of the Lord
B. J. Beu

COLOR
White

SCRIPTURE READINGS
Isaiah 43:1-7; Psalm 29; Acts 8:14-17; Luke 3:15-17, 21-22

THEME IDEAS
The power to protect and redeem Israel (Isaiah 43) is seen in new and vital ways through the giving of the Holy Spirit (Acts 8 and Luke 3). The people God called by name, the people God accompanied through fire and water, have been given a new blessing—the power of God's very Spirit. This blessing is not just for the Jews, but also for Samaritans and all those who accept Jesus as the messiah, the chosen one of God. With this blessing, however, comes judgment. The righteous will be gathered to God like wheat to the granary, but the unrighteous will go like chaff to unquenchable fire. The power of the living God to bring peace (Psalm 29) is the same power to bring calamity on the unrighteous. These readings warn us against being cavalier about our baptism or the awesome power of God's Holy Spirit.

CALL TO WORSHIP (PSALM 29, ISAIAH 43)

Sing praises to the Lord.
Sing of God's glory and strength.
God calls to us over the waters.
God strengthens us for the journey.
Sing praises to the Lord.
Sing of God's glory and strength.
The waters of our baptism cleanse us.
The waters of renewal heal our wounds.
Sing praises to the Lord.
Sing of God's glory and strength.
We have come to worship the Lord.
We have come to sing God's praise.

CALL TO WORSHIP (LUKE 3)

People of God, do you know who you are?
We are God's beloved children.
Disciples of Christ, do you know who you are?
We are God's beloved children.
Heirs of the Holy Spirit, do you know who you are?
We are God's beloved children.
Sealed in God's love, through the waters of our baptism,
let us worship the living God.

CONTEMPORARY GATHERING WORDS
(PSALM 29, ISAIAH 43, LUKE 3)

Who is like our God—
the One who thunders over the waters?
Who is like the Lord—
the One who sits enthroned in glory?
Who is like our God—
the One whose winnowing fork
scatters the unrighteous?
Who is like the Lord—
the One who leads the people through the sea?
Come worship the One who seals us in baptism,
and saves us from our sins.

CONTEMPORARY GATHERING WORDS (LUKE 3)

Why have you come here?
We seek the cleansing waters of baptism.
What do you hope to find?
We seek God's forgiveness.
Will you receive the Holy Spirit
with gratitude and praise?
Our hearts are open to Christ's Spirit,
ready to be born anew.
Receive God's Spirit.
Alleluia!

PRAISE SENTENCES (PSALM 29)

God is great!
Sing glory to our God!
The Lord is mighty!
Shout praises to the Lord!
God is enthroned forever!
Praise God!

PRAISE SENTENCES (ACTS 8)

God's Spirit is upon us!
God's Spirit washes over us!
God's Spirit is upon us!
God's Spirit washes over us!

OPENING PRAYER (ISAIAH 43, ACTS 8)

Beloved One,
you call us by name
and claim us as your own.
As we were sealed into your love
by the waters of our baptism,
claim us once again
through the power of your Holy Spirit.
May your glory shine forth
in everything we do,

that the world might know
we are a people of the water
and of the Spirit. Amen.

OPENING PRAYER (LUKE 3, ACTS 8)

Divine Spirit,
descend upon us this day,
as you descended upon Jesus
on the day of his baptism.
Heal our brokenness,
and seal us once again
into the fullness of your love.
May we continue to swim
in the cleansing waters of our baptism,
and may we be known
as people of the water,
and of your Spirit. Amen.

BENEDICTION (ISAIAH 43)

Hear the good news:
God calls us by name
and fashions us for glory.
Through the waters of our baptism,
we have been washed clean
and raised to newness of life.
Hear the good news:
the Holy Spirit blesses us
and seals us in God's love.
We go forth as people blessed by God,
that we might be a blessing to others.

BENEDICTION (ISAIAH 43, ACTS 8, LUKE 3)

God has called us by name,
inviting us into new life in Christ.
We are a people of the water,
baptized as disciples of Christ.

God has called us by name,
bestowing upon us the blessings
of the Holy Spirit.
   We are a people of the water,
   baptized through the power of God's Spirit.
Go with the blessings of God.

JANUARY 14, 2007

Second Sunday after the Epiphany
Erik J. Alsgaard

COLOR
Green

SCRIPTURE READINGS
Isaiah 62:1-5; Psalm 36:5-10; 1 Corinthians 12:1-11; John 2:1-11

THEME IDEAS
God's grace and love are bright and shining gifts to a dark and hurting world. We find this echoed in today's readings: "Your steadfast love ... *extends* to the heavens" (Psalm 36:5); "You shall be a *crown* of beauty in the hand of the LORD, / and a royal diadem in the hand of your God" (Isaiah 62:3); "Jesus ... *revealed* his glory" (John 2:11). God's love is made manifest in many ways, including the gifts of the Spirit, as mentioned in the Corinthians reading. Our worship today should show how members of Christ's body, the church, bring forth God's love.

CALL TO WORSHIP (1 CORINTHIANS 12)
There are many gifts, talents, and abilities given by God.
But there is only one Spirit.
There are a variety of things we can do to serve the Lord.
But it is the same Lord we all serve.
There are many activities we can do to serve God:

10

teach, sing, clean, preach, play, work ...
But all these are activated by God.
There are many manifestations of God's Spirit
in the world.
It is impossible to list them all.
To say that one is better than another is foolish.
God gives to each as God chooses.
Thanks be to God!

CALL TO WORSHIP (PSALM 36)

No matter how far we wander from you, O God,
your steadfast love finds us.
No matter how unjust the world seems to us, O God,
your steadfast righteousness sustains us.
No matter how vulnerable our lives seem to us, O God,
your steadfast presence gives us hope.
No matter how unloved and uncared for we feel, O God,
you hear our cries and answer our prayers.
Thanks be to God!

CONTEMPORARY GATHERING WORDS
(ISAIAH 62, JOHN 2)

With God, all things are made new.
We are made new creatures in Christ!
The mouth of the Lord has spoken.
We are made new creatures in Christ!
The old things have passed away.
We are made new creatures in Christ!

PRAISE SENTENCES

We lift up our voices in praise.
God's steadfast love never fails.

OPENING PRAYER

Gracious and loving God,
source of all wholeness, forgiveness, and mercy,
may your Spirit

    heal those who are torn,
    mend those who are broken,
    and protect those who are fragile.
Enable us, O God,
    through the gift of your steadfast love,
    to remember who we are
    and whose we are.
In your love,
    may we be true and faithful disciples
    of your Son, Jesus Christ our Lord,
    in whose name we pray. Amen.

OPENING PRAYER (1 CORINTHIANS 12)

God of all good gifts,
    we thank you and praise you.
Your Spirit has touched our lives,
    bringing wisdom, ability, strength, courage,
    and passion.
Enable us to use our gifts
    in service to you and to others.
In all that we do,
    and in all that we are,
    may your name be glorified,
    that your kingdom will be with us
    and reside here on this earth.
We pray this in the name of your Son,
    our Lord, Jesus Christ. Amen.

UNISON PRAYER OR PRAYER OF CONFESSION (JOHN 2)

Lord, we need a miracle today.
Like Jesus changing water into wine
    at the wedding feast in Cana,
    we need a miracle today.
We are tired, Lord, of the hurts of this world.
We are discouraged

in the face of injustice, war, poverty, and indifference.
We need a miracle today, Lord.
Your steadfast love, like a mighty mountain,
    will not be moved.
Your gifts, as many as the mighty winds,
    cannot be counted.
Your glory, like a mighty torch,
    will not be put out.
Lord, crown us with your love.
Show us your glory,
    that in you we may be moved
        to acts of kindness, love, justice, and mercy.
Lord, we need a miracle today. Amen.

BENEDICTION

And now, from the One who is indeed the giver
    of all good gifts:
        go and share what God has given you;
        go and proclaim that God's love is here;
        go in the power of God's Spirit
            to make all things new.

BENEDICTION (PSALM 36, 1 CORINTHIANS 12)

Drink deep of God's love.
    God's love endures forever!
Drink deep of God's Spirit.
    God's Spirit endures forever!
Feast on the abundance of God's gifts.
    God's gifts never end!

JANUARY 21, 2007

Third Sunday after the Epiphany
Joanne Carlson Brown

COLOR
Green

SCRIPTURE READINGS
Nehemiah 8:1-3, 5-6, 8-10; Psalm 19; 1 Corinthians 12:12-31a; Luke 4:14-21

THEME IDEAS
At first glance, these readings don't set forth one overarching theme. But the issue of ministry is woven throughout. Jesus' understanding of his ministry, articulated at its beginning, echoes the grand themes of the law, which are celebrated in both the Nehemiah and Psalms texts. Ministry calls for many types of people and gifts, but all these are joined together as the body of Christ, as Paul affirms in 1 Corinthians. We are bound together by the gift and the precepts of the law, which guide our understanding and practice of ministry.

CALL TO WORSHIP (NEHEMIAH 8, PSALM 19)
Come before your God with praise and thanksgiving.
The joy of God is our strength.
Join with the heavens and the earth
in telling the goodness of our God.
The joy of God is our strength.
Come let us worship God, who revives our souls.

14

CALL TO WORSHIP (LUKE 4, 1 CORINTHIANS 12)

The Spirit of God is upon us.
We are called to be God's people.
The Spirit of God is upon us.
We are called to be the body of Christ.
Come let us worship God, who binds us together
in love and service.

CONTEMPORARY GATHERING WORDS (1 CORINTHIANS 12)

Whoever you are, you are welcome.
That is good news!
Bring your gifts to praise God.
We are happy to be together.
Let us worship God with joy and spirit.

PRAISE SENTENCES (NEHEMIAH 8, 1 CORINTHIANS 12)

The Spirit of God is upon us!
This is a holy day and we are a holy people!
The joy of God is our strength!
All of us, with all our gifts, we are the body of Christ!

OPENING PRAYER (1 CORINTHIANS 12, LUKE 4)

Bountiful God,
  you have blessed us with so many gifts.
In this time of worship,
  may we be open to receiving these gifts.
Help us claim our gifts
  and use them to bring liberation and justice
    to a hurting world.
May the words of our mouths,
  and the meditations of our hearts,
  be acceptable to you.
May the transforming Spirit of joy and unity

bind us together as your body,
that we may be your hands and feet and voice
in this, your world. Amen.

OPENING PRAYER (NEHEMIAH 8, 1 CORINTHIANS 12, LUKE 4)
O wondrous God,
on this holy day,
we have gathered together once again
to celebrate your presence among us,
to praise you, and to thank you
for all you have given us.
May this time of worship
strengthen and refresh us,
and fill us with such joy
that we cannot help but share it
with everyone around us.
Though we are very different people,
with many different talents and gifts,
make us one in your Spirit,
that we may be your ministers
in the world. Amen.

PRAYER OF CONFESSION (NEHEMIAH 8, PSALM 19, 1 CORINTHIANS 12, LUKE 4)
Ever present One,
you call us to be your presence,
your body in this world,
but too often we get caught up
in being a hand or a foot,
and lose sight of the overarching mission
you set before us.
We fracture into pieces.
We go our separate ways,
forgetting we need each other to be whole.
You have given us your law to be our guide,

but we turn our backs
  on what we see as rules and restrictions,
   fearful that we will not live up to your expectations.
Help us see with new eyes,
 and hear with the ears of our heart,
 the liberating spirit of the law
  that strengthens and revives and enables us
   to be and do all you call us to be and do.
O God of liberation and justice,
 help us be faithful witnesses
  to your law of love and unity. Amen.

WORDS OF ASSURANCE (LUKE 4)

The Spirit of God is upon us.
God has called us to bring good news and liberation
 to the poor, to the marginalized,
 and to all who are in need anywhere.
God's joy is our strength.
Through God we can do all things.
God's Spirit surrounds us with forgiveness and love.

PRAYER BEFORE SERMON

May the words of my mouth,
 and the meditation of our hearts,
 be acceptable in your sight,
 our Rock and our Redeemer.

BENEDICTION (1 CORINTHIANS 12, LUKE 4)

You have been called and anointed.
You have been strengthened and enlightened.
You have become one body in Christ.
Now go to spread joy and liberation
 in word and in deed
  to all the world.

BENEDICTION (1 CORINTHIANS 12, LUKE 4)
The Spirit of God is upon you.
We go forth proclaiming God's love and liberation.
The Spirit of Christ is upon you.
We go forth to live lives of justice and freedom.
The power of the Spirit is upon you.
We go forth as one body, one spirit,
one witness to the promises of our God.

JANUARY 28, 2007

Fourth Sunday after the Epiphany
Mary J. Scifres

COLOR
Green

SCRIPTURE READINGS
Jeremiah 1:4-10; Psalm 71:1-6; 1 Corinthians 13:1-13; Luke 4:21-30

THEME IDEAS
The challenge of discipleship flows through all of today's readings. Jeremiah's vivid call to ministry, coupled with the psalmist's inspiring words, remind us of God's hand in our lives, regardless of our knowledge of God's presence. Jesus' experience in Luke 4 is a shocking portrayal of the harshness of life as a follower of God. Proclaiming God's truth is neither simple, nor safe. Even the beloved words of the Corinthians "love chapter" are filled with challenges to endure hardships and to believe when trust is betrayed. Following Christ and answering God's call are challenging tasks indeed!

CALL TO WORSHIP (PSALM 71)
Come into God's presence, our Rock and our Refuge.
We come as God's children, ready and willing.
Know that the Lord has called us here.
God has called us to worship, to love, and to serve.

19

Praises we sing to the Hope of our world.
Salvation we proclaim, for one and for all.
Come into God's presence, our Rock and our Refuge.
We come as Christ's children, God's praises to sing.

CALL TO WORSHIP (JEREMIAH 1, 1 CORINTHIANS 13)

The word of God comes into our lives,
calling and urging us on.
God's word calls us now, opening our eyes,
and showing us pathways of service and love.
The word of God calls us to worship and praise,
strengthening our journeys of faith.
We worship with faith, opening our hearts
and our minds.
May God bless us with faith, hope, and love.

CALL TO WORSHIP (JEREMIAH 1, PSALM 71, 1 CORINTHIANS 13)

Worship the Lord, the God of heaven and earth!
Praise be to our Refuge and Strength!
God of faith, God of hope, God of love,
we come with prayers of joy and of fear.
May your love be our guide.
May your hope be in us.
God of our faith, bring us closer to Christ.

CONTEMPORARY GATHERING WORDS (1 CORINTHIANS 13)

Love has welcomed us here.
Let love be our guiding light.
Love is all around.
Let love be our guiding light.
Love is patient and kind.
Let love be our guiding light.

Love has welcomed us here.
Let love be our guiding light.

PRAISE SENTENCES (PSALM 71)

The Lord is our Rock, our Refuge, and our Strength.
Praise be to God our Rock!
The Lord is our Rock, our Refuge, and our Strength.
Praise be to God our Rock!

OPENING PRAYER (1 CORINTHIANS 13)

God of hope and love,
let your love shine upon us this day.
Let your patience and kindness flow through us,
inspiring us to new depths of love and hope.
Transform our love,
that we might overcome envy and resentment,
and rejoice in justice and righteousness.
Envelop us in your love,
that believing, hoping, and enduring
may become our way of life
on the path of love.
In loving hope, we pray. Amen.

OPENING PRAYER (JEREMIAH 1)

God of wisdom and power,
speak to us this day.
Open our ears and our minds
to hear your words.
Awaken our hearts
to respond with love.
Inspire our actions,
that we might serve others
with confidence and commitment.
In the name of the One
who created and called us, amen.

PRAYER OF CONFESSION (LUKE 4)

Gracious God,
    be with us as we walk
      through the hills and valleys of life.
Give us courage
    to face trials and tribulations.
Forgive us
    when we avoid the challenges
      and struggles of discipleship.
Grant us wisdom
    to proclaim your word
      and live your love.
And guide us into paths of peace.
In Jesus' name, we pray. Amen.

WORDS OF ASSURANCE (PSALM 71)

Christ Jesus, our Rock and our Refuge,
    is walking with us even now.
Through God's powerful love and gracious salvation,
    we are forgiven and renewed.
Know that the God of hope
    is with us today and always.

BENEDICTION (1 CORINTHIANS 13)

Go as God's love into the world,
    bearing burdens and enduring challenges.
Go as Christ's children into the world,
    hoping for goodness and believing in miracles.
Go with the Spirit into the world,
    letting love be your guide.
    We are God's love to the world!

BENEDICTION (1 CORINTHIANS 13)

And now, my friends,
    we have received three gifts:
      faith, hope, and love.

Go with faith.
Go with hope.
But most of all
   go with love,
      for this is God's greatest gift!

FEBRUARY 4, 2007

Fifth Sunday after the Epiphany

B. J. Beu

COLOR
Green

SCRIPTURE READINGS
Isaiah 6:1-8 (9-13); Psalm 138; 1 Corinthians 15:1-11; Luke 5:1-11

THEME IDEAS
Isaiah's face-to-face encounter with the Lord of hosts evokes the same response as Peter's encounter with Jesus on the water: they both feel unworthy to be in the awesome and fearful presence of God's holiness. Yet, despite these feelings of inadequacy, when faced with God's call, we are ultimately charged to respond with Isaiah: "Here I am; send me!" Today's readings include contrasting proclamations from God: messages of woe and destruction (Isaiah 6) are conjoined with messages of hope and salvation (Psalm 138, 1 Corinthians 15, and Luke 5). Whether we are in situations of destruction or reclamation, however, our proper response is to worship the One who brings life out of death and hope out of despair.

CALL TO WORSHIP (PSALM 138)
Give thanks to the Lord.
Sing praises to our God.

We bow before the Holy One,
with steadfast love and faithfulness.
Call to the Lord.
Seek God with your whole heart.
The Lord is steadfast and true.
God's promises endure forever.
Give thanks to the Lord.
Sing praises to our God.
We bow before the Holy One,
with steadfast love and faithfulness.

CALL TO WORSHIP (ISAIAH 6)

The voice of God is calling:
"Whom shall I send?"
We are here to answer God's call.
The voice of God is calling:
"Who will be my faithful disciple?"
We are here to answer God's call.
The voice of God is calling:
"Who will go and be a light to the nations?"
We are here to answer God's call:
"Here I am. Send me!"

CONTEMPORARY GATHERING WORDS (ISAIAH 6, LUKE 5)

Have you not heard?
God has work for us to do.
But we are not worthy.
Have you not heard?
God has plans for us.
But we are not ready.
Have you not heard?
Through God, all things are possible.
We will put our trust in God.

Contemporary Gathering Words (Psalm 138)

Thank the Lord with hearts full of love.
Our hearts overflow with love.
Sing to the Lord with hearts full of joy.
Our hearts overflow with joy.
Walk with the Lord with hearts free from fear.
Our hearts overflow with the peace of God.
Worship the Lord with hearts touched by the Holy Spirit.
Our hearts overflow with God's blessings.

Praise Sentences (Isaiah 6)

Our God sits on the throne,
    surrounded by the heavenly host.
Sing holy, holy, holy!
Our God sits on the throne,
    robed with power and might.
Sing holy, holy, holy!
Our God sits on the throne,
    worthy of our worship and praise.
Sing holy, holy, holy!

Praise Sentences (1 Corinthians 15)

Praise the One who died to save us from our sins!
Christ is greatly to be praised!
Praise the One who rose from the dead
to bring us everlasting life!
Christ is greatly to be praised!
Praise the One who calls us to be the church!
Christ is greatly to be praised!

Opening Prayer (Luke 5, Isaiah 6)

Holy Mystery,
    your wisdom is as deep as the sea,
    your power as vast as the starry skies.
Do not hide your face from us,
    but call us from the wreckage of our lives.

Grant us courage,
    that we might hear your call
        and leave the safety of shallow waters.
Help us face our fears,
    that we might bravely follow you
        wherever you might lead.
Save us from aimlessness and sin, O God,
    that we might be sure-footed on the journey. Amen.

PRAYER OF CONFESSION (ISAIAH 6, LUKE 5)

Almighty God,
    we are a people of unclean lips,
        more accustomed to spreading gossip
            than to singing "Holy, holy, holy"
                with the heavenly hosts.
Breathe your Holy Spirit in us anew.
Wash away our sin,
    and we will be made clean.
Call to us, and we will follow you.
As the disciples left their fishing boats
    and set out for new shores,
        may we too become fishers of men and women,
            that all people might be brought to your glory
                in Jesus' name. Amen.

ASSURANCE OF PARDON (ISAIAH 6, LUKE 5)

Hear the good news:
    through forgiveness in Christ,
    our guilt has departed
        and our sins have been blotted out.
Thanks be to God!

BENEDICTION (PSALM 138, 1 CORINTHIANS 15)

God is our strength.
    God's steadfast love endures forever.
God is our hope.

God's steadfast love endures forever.
God is our salvation.
God's steadfast love endures forever.

BENEDICTION (1 CORINTHIANS 15, LUKE 5)
Called as Christ's disciples ...
we follow our risen Lord.
Called as Christ's disciples ...
we are guided by the saints.
Called as Christ's disciples ...
we are blessed by the living God.

BENEDICTION (LUKE 5)
Do not fear the waters of faith.
Christ is with us in the boat.
Do not fear the dangers of the deep.
God is with us on the journey.
Do not fear casting your nets among the lost.
God will grant us a bountiful catch.
Thanks be to God!

FEBRUARY 11, 2007

Sixth Sunday after the Epiphany
Jamie Greening

COLOR
Green

SCRIPTURE READINGS
Jeremiah 17:5-10; Psalm 1; 1 Corinthians 15:12-20; Luke 6:17-26

THEME IDEAS
Psalm 1 and Jeremiah 17 share a depiction of trees planted by streams of water, inviting thematic explorations of discipleship and personal growth, as well as perseverance in hard times (think fruit and harvest). There is a strong resurrection emphasis from the epistle passage, allowing a bridge from resurrection light to Lent's coming darkness and fasting. Luke's Sermon on the Plain brings ethical considerations and could be compared with Matthew's more familiar Sermon on the Mount. It is a good text to address social action/justice and Christian responsibility.

CALL TO WORSHIP (JEREMIAH 17, PSALM 1)
Teach us, O Lord, to be faithful,
like a strong tree growing in the desert sun.
Let our roots run deep to the sweet waters
of your Holy Spirit—

to resist the heat of sin,
to yield the fruit of the Spirit in our daily lives,
to be free from worry about trivial things,
to wither not from doubt,
to delight in your laws.
Teach us, O Lord, to be faithful,
like a strong tree growing in the desert sun.

CALL TO WORSHIP (LUKE 6)
Blessed are those in poverty,
for theirs is the kingdom of God.
Blessed are those who hunger,
for they will have food to eat.
Blessed are those who weep from abuse,
for they will laugh again.
Blessed are those who are hated
and rejected for Christ's sake,
for they will be blessed by God.
Blessed are we who have gathered here
in God's presence,
for together we are the people of God.

CONTEMPORARY GATHERING WORDS (1 CORINTHIANS 15)
Christ has been raised from the dead.
He is risen indeed.
Christ is victorious over the grave.
He is risen indeed.
Christ has defeated the powers of death.
He is risen indeed.

PRAISE SENTENCES (LUKE 6)
Give glory to Jesus,
who cares for the poor
and loves the hungry.
Give glory to the Holy Spirit,

who turns our weeping into joy.
Give glory to Almighty God,
    who vindicates the oppressed.
What a wonderful triune Lord we serve.

OPENING PRAYER (PSALM 1)

Lord,
    delighting in your law
        does not come natural to us.
As we worship you today,
    help us meditate upon your words of life.
We have come to plant our roots
    into the stream of your living waters.
May the fruit of our worship blossom
    as a sweet offering to you. Amen.

OPENING PRAYER (1 CORINTHIANS 15, LUKE 6)

Holy God,
    we cling to the light and power
        of the resurrection we find in your Son,
        and our Savior, Christ Jesus.
We know that if he has not been raised,
    then there is no hope—
        no hope for the poor, the hungry, or the oppressed;
        no hope for the rejected, or for those who mourn.
But because your Son has indeed been raised,
    we have hope and know that we are blessed—
        blessed with spiritual richness;
        blessed with the bread of life;
        blessed with the laughter of true joy;
        and blessed with liberation from fear. Amen.

PRAYER OF CONFESSION (JEREMIAH 17, PSALM 1)

In the midst of winter's cold,
we acknowledge our hardness of heart.
Have mercy upon us, O God.

We have listened to sinners.
We have made a mockery of peace.
We have blown with the winds of popular opinion.
We have trusted in petty people.
We are blind to our prosperity
and covet the wealth of others.
We have chosen the barren wasteland of isolation.
We have neglected our community.
Lord have mercy.

ASSURANCE OF PARDON

We cling to your grace,
and trust your forgiveness.
In Christ's forgiveness,
we find the path to eternal life. Amen.

BENEDICTION (PSALM 1)

The Lord watches over the way of the righteous,
but the way of the wicked will perish.
Let us leave this place to travel the paths of righteousness.
Blessed are those who walk in righteousness.

BENEDICTION (JEREMIAH 17)

May the Lord search our hearts,
and examine our minds, and find only goodness.
May we leave this place
and receive the reward of God's blessings
in every part of our lives.

FEBRUARY 18, 2007

Transfiguration Sunday
Bryan Schneider-Thomas

COLOR
White

SCRIPTURE READINGS
Exodus 34:29-35; Psalm 99; 2 Corinthians 3:12–4:2; Luke 9:28-36 (37-43*a*)

THEME IDEAS
Transfiguration Sunday is one of the minor festivals. Being the last Sunday before Lent, it serves as a transition from the revelations of Epiphany and the following days, to the reflection of Lent. In the gospel lesson, Jesus is discussing his departure with Moses and Elijah. While it is appropriate for this day to begin looking toward Jerusalem, it is still primarily a day of celebration in which we glimpse the glory of God in Jesus Christ. It is still a Sunday of revelation and celebration, filled with light and glory—themes present in all of today's readings. If the glory of Christ is used as a primary theme, it may be desirable to expand the 2 Corinthians reading to include the first part of chapter 12.

CALL TO WORSHIP (PSALM 99)
God is above all things, exalted and worthy of praise.
Praise God! Holy and mighty is the Lord our God.

God is a mighty ruler who loves justice,
establishes equity, and cherishes righteousness.
Praise God! Holy and mighty is the Lord our God.
God is full of glory, a radiant sun, more splendid
than all creation.
Praise God! Holy and mighty is the Lord our God.

CALL TO WORSHIP (EXODUS 34, 2 CORINTHIANS 3–4, LUKE 9)

Moses came down from Mount Sinai,
and his face glowed from beholding God's glory.
Jesus went up the mountain, and Peter, James,
and John saw his appearance glow with God's glory.
The people were frightened by Moses' appearance.
The disciples were baffled by Jesus' appearance.
Moses hid his face from the people with a veil
so they would not be frightened.
From a cloud, a voice called to the disciples:
"This is my Son, my Chosen; listen to him!"
In the Glory of God, Paul tells us to act with great
boldness.
"And all of us, with unveiled faces, seeing the
glory of the Lord as though reflected in a mirror,
are being transformed into the same image
from one degree of glory to another;
for this comes from the Lord, the Spirit."

CONTEMPORARY GATHERING WORDS

Come into the presence of God.
Come look for the radiance of Christ.
Come be transformed by divine glory,
and let others see God in your face.

PRAISE SENTENCES (PSALM 99)

God is ruler over all the earth.
Let the people praise God's awesome name.
Our God loves justice, establishes equity,

and is our source of righteousness.
Holy is God!

PRAISE SENTENCES

At Jesus' birth, there were shepherds in the fields,
   and the "glory of the Lord shone around them"
   (Luke 2:9*b*).
Simeon, guided by the Spirit, saw Jesus:
   "a light to reveal God ... the glory of your people"
   (Luke 2:32 NLT).
On a mountain, Jesus was transfigured
   and the disciples "saw his glory" (Luke 9:32*b*).
When Jesus returns, he promises that all will see him
   "with power and great glory" (Luke 21:27*b*).
So stand up with all confidence for by the Spirit
   you are "being transformed into the same image
   from one degree of glory to another"
   (2 Corinthians 3:18*b*).

OPENING PRAYER (LUKE 9)

Holy God, parent of all humankind,
   at Jesus' baptism, you called your Son beloved
      and announced your pleasure in him.
After his transfiguration,
   you commended your Son again,
   and told those present to listen to him.
Help us listen to him once more,
   proclaiming the love
      that makes us all your children. Amen.

OPENING PRAYER (LUKE 9)

Glorious Christ,
   we long to see your splendor
      and be transformed by your majesty.
Open our eyes,
   that we might see your presence
      face to face. Amen.

PRAYER OF CONFESSION (EXODUS 34, 2 CORINTHIANS 3–4)

Almighty God,
you come to us and reveal yourself
through your Son, Jesus Christ.
In his glory we are made new.
Yet we often respond with fear,
rather than with enthusiasm,
when we look upon your presence.
Forgive our hesitancy
to serve you bravely and joyfully.
Teach us how to serve with boldness,
and transform us into glory—
glory we behold in the transfiguration of Jesus.
Amen.

ASSURANCE OF PARDON

Do not lose heart.
By God's mercy we are forgiven
and equipped for our ministry.
Through the grace of Jesus Christ,
you are forgiven.

BENEDICTION

Face to face, we have seen the glory of God,
and we are transformed.
Face to face, we show the glory of God,
and others are transformed.
Go to serve God and others in all that you do.

BENEDICTION (2 CORINTHIANS 3–4)

Filled with the hope and glory of Jesus Christ,
walk with boldness.
Do not lose heart
when engaged in the ministry of God,
for God is with you.

FEBRUARY 21, 2007

Ash Wednesday
John A. Brewer

COLOR
Purple or Gray

SCRIPTURE READINGS
Joel 2:1-2, 12-17; Psalm 51:1-17; 2 Corinthians 5:20b–6:10; Matthew 6:1-6, 16-21

THEME IDEAS
In the sense that Advent is about "anticipation," Lent is about "realization." Grasping the existential reality of Jesus' suffering and passion, and knowing that his compassionate acts of sacrifice were *personal,* can be life-changing for the Lenten pilgrim. Lent is not about the future, as is the case in Advent. It is not about the past, either. Lent is about the personal impact Jesus is having on our life and behavior, right here, right now. It is the understanding of judgment (Joel) that comes with the crucifixion of Christ. This understanding calls us to our own "reality check," illuminating our selfish, materialistic, insensitive character. Over the drone of busyness, we can barely hear the call of God to "return" or to "draw near the throne of grace." This is a season to "get real and honest" in our relationship with God.

CALL TO WORSHIP (PSALM 51, NIV)

Have mercy on me, O God,
according to your unfailing love.
According to your great compassion
blot out my transgressions.
Wash away all my iniquity
and cleanse me from my sin....
Surely you desire truth in the inner parts;
you teach me wisdom in the inmost place.
Cleanse me with hyssop, and I will be clean.
Wash me, and I will be whiter than snow....
Create in me a pure heart, O God,
and renew a steadfast spirit within me.

CALL TO WORSHIP (2 CORINTHIANS 5, PSALM 51, JOEL 2 NIV)

(Response may be sung as a Kyrie Eleison)
I tell you, now is the time of God's favor.
Now is the day of salvation.
Lord, have mercy.
Christ, have mercy.
Lord, have mercy.
He who had no sin, was made to be sin for us,
that in him we might become the righteousness of God.
Lord, have mercy.
Christ, have mercy.
Lord, have mercy.
Rend your heart and not your garments.
Return to the Lord your God.
Lord, have mercy.
Christ, have mercy.
Lord, have mercy.
For God is gracious and compassionate,
slow to anger and abounding in love.
Lord, have mercy.
Christ, have mercy.
Lord, have mercy.

CONTEMPORARY GATHERING WORDS

You are the one I saw standing in the shadows,
aren't you?
Leave me alone. I don't want to be seen.
Come on over here. Come let this Light
wash away the wounds of the dark places in your life.
Leave me alone. I want to do this on my own.
And you, didn't I see you the other day
in that exclusive clothing shop at the mall?
Leave me alone. I just needed something new
to wear to our community banquet for the poor.
Come here. Come and learn how to store up treasures
that will not grow old, nor succumb to the ravages
of time.
Leave me alone. I need to trust in my own wealth.
And you, aren't you the one who is always hogging
the limelight at your church leadership meetings?
Leave me alone. Someone has to take responsibility.
Come here. You are too easily satisfied with the rewards
of recognition. Let me introduce you to the living God,
who will reward you in secret for the service you give
in secret.

PRAISE SENTENCES

The earth is the Lord's, and everything in it,
    the world, and all who live in it (based on Psalm 24:1).
The Lord reigns.
The Lord is robed in majesty
    and is armed with strength (based on Psalm 93:1).
Within your temple, O God,
    we meditate on your unfailing love.
Like your name, O God,
    your praise reaches to the ends of the earth
    (based on Psalm 48:9-10).

OPENING PRAYER

O God of endless mercy,
    we gather on this day

to acknowledge our mortality,
and our complete reliance on you
for compassion and forgiveness.
If there is any hope for us, O God,
our hope rests completely in you.
Have mercy, O God, have mercy.
You are the source of our mortal life.
You are the source of our spiritual life.
You are the destiny to whom we return
in the hope of Jesus Christ,
our risen Lord and Savior.
May the mark of mortality
remind us of our dust-to-dust existence,
and draw us nearer to you. Amen.

OPENING PRAYER OR PRAYER OF CONFESSION

O God, our Creator,
O Christ, our Rabbi,
O Holy Spirit, our Power of transformation,
may we know your very real presence
on this night.
As we bow before your presence,
remove from us any pretense
of being other than we are.
With brutal honesty,
bring us to terms with ourselves.
In your presence,
may your Light reveal the shame and guilt
we seek to hide from you.
In your presence,
may we be confronted with your calling
to lead holy lives on this earth.
Help us, O God, to return to you.
Only then can we know
the peace and possibilities
you have in store for us.

We humble ourselves in your sight, O God,
  for you know us completely
  and call us to be more than we have become.
Lord have mercy. Amen.

PRAYER OF CONFESSION

O God of great mercy,
  have compassion upon us this day.
Forgive us,
  for we have sinned against you.
Even though we try to hide our sins,
  even though we live in denial
  of our greatest need,
  you know us altogether and completely.
Bring us out from the shadows,
  and let your light shine upon us.
Reveal to us our need for repentance and renewal.
Fill us with the weight of your love
  until we come to our knees in honest humility.
We need you, O God.
We need your wisdom.
We need your patience.
We need a new beginning—
  a beginning that you alone can offer.
O God of great mercy,
  have compassion upon us this day.
May Christ work in us and through us. Amen.

ASSURANCE OF PARDON (JOHN 3:17 KJV)

God sent not his Son into the world
  to condemn the world;
  but that the world through him
    might be saved.

BENEDICTION (DEUTERONOMY 6:4)

Hear, O Israel: The Lord our God, the Lord is one.
Love the Lord your God with all your heart
  and with all your soul and with all your strength.

BENEDICTION

Go forth from this sacred space
and know that God goes before you.
From before your birth, and long after your death,
you are in a constant and real relationship
with your loving, forgiving, encouraging God.
Live as children of the Light,
in the name of Christ. Amen.

FEBRUARY 25, 2007

First Sunday in Lent
B. J. Beu

COLOR
Purple

SCRIPTURE READINGS
Deuteronomy 26:1-11; Psalm 91:1-2, 9-16; Romans 10:8*b*-13; Luke 4:1-13

THEME IDEAS
Salvation comes from God. This theme runs through each of today's readings. With a call to remember how God freed the Hebrew people from bondage in Egypt, Deuteronomy records the fulfillment of God's promise to bring Israel into the Promised Land. The psalmist rejoices that God blesses the faithful with refuge and strength. In Romans, Paul promises salvation to all who believe in Christ Jesus with their hearts and profess this belief with their lips, whether they be Gentile or Jew. In Luke, Jesus is tempted by the devil after fasting in the wilderness. Jesus resists the devil's temptations by putting God's priorities ahead of human calculations.

CALL TO WORSHIP (PSALM 91, ROMANS 10)
Let us worship God, our fortress and our refuge.
In God we dwell secure. Alleluia!
Let us worship God, who delivers us from evil.

In God we dwell secure. Alleluia!
Let us worship God, who justifies our faith.
In God we dwell secure. Alleluia!

CALL TO WORSHIP (DEUTERONOMY 26, ROMANS 10)

We are blessed by the promises God made
to our ancestors.
We dwell in a land flowing with milk and honey.
We are encouraged by the promises God made
to the prophets.
**Everyone who calls on the name of the Lord
will be saved.**
We are called here by the promises of God.
Let us worship with thanksgiving and praise.

CONTEMPORARY GATHERING WORDS (ROMANS 10)

Call on the name of the Lord and be saved!
We confess Jesus with our lips.
Believe in the name of the Lord and be saved!
We believe in Jesus with all our hearts.
Live as disciples of Jesus and be saved!
**We will live and worship,
blessed and redeemed by our living savior.**

CONTEMPORARY GATHERING WORDS (PSALM 91)

Disasters strike.
Where can we go?
God is always there.
Enemies surround us.
Whom can we trust?
God is always there.
Life can be hard.
Who can ease the load?
God is always there.

PRAISE SENTENCES (ROMANS 10)
God raised Jesus from the dead!
Jesus is Lord!
Jesus is Lord!
Jesus is Lord!

PRAISE SENTENCES (ROMANS 10)
Jesus is Lord!
Our lips worship you, O God!
Jesus rose from the dead!
Our hearts love you, O God!
Jesus is the Lord of life!
Our lives are offered to you, O God!

OPENING PRAYER (LUKE 4)
Merciful God,
　　your ways lead to life,
　　your light shines in our darkness.
Strengthen us in our weakness—
　　for so many things tempt us,
　　so many misplaced priorities
　　　　distract our attention from you.
Help us value your enduring word
　　over comforts that do not endure.
Help us choose lives of service
　　over opportunities to be served.
May we be worthy of our calling,
　　that we might aid others
　　　　who have lost their way. Amen.

OFFERTORY PRAYER (DEUTERONOMY 26)
Mighty God,
　　when we were slaves in Egypt,
　　　　you rescued us with a mighty hand
　　　　and an outstretched arm.
With signs and wonders,

you led us into a land
   flowing with milk and honey.
We come to you today,
   thankful for your manifold blessings.
Receive these offerings
   as the first fruits
      of all that you have given us. Amen.

BENEDICTION (PSALM 91)

Abide in the shadow of the Most High
   God is our refuge and our strength.
Put your trust in the Holy One.
   God is our fortress against the storm.
Call on the name of the Lord.
   God is our salvation.
Go with God's blessing.

BENEDICTION (ROMANS 10)

Rejoice, people of God, for everyone who calls
on the name of the Lord shall be saved.
   We rejoice in Christ our Savior!
Go forth with God's blessings.

MARCH 4, 2007

Second Sunday in Lent
Mary Petrina Boyd

COLOR

Purple

SCRIPTURE READINGS

Genesis 15:1-12, 17-18; Psalm 27; Philippians 3:17–4:1;
Luke 13:31-35

THEME IDEAS

The Scriptures proclaim God's faithfulness and the security that is found in God's love. God's promises are true,
and God's blessings are abundant. God is faithful to the
covenant, bringing new life in unlikely places. God is creator of all, from the stars in the heavens to the tiniest chick.
God rejects evil, promising glory to the faithful. Faced
with threats to his life, Jesus reaches out with compassion.

CALL TO WORSHIP (PSALM 27)

The Lord is our light and our strength.
Whom shall we fear?
The Lord is the stronghold of our lives.
Of whom shall we be afraid?
Trust in the Lord at all times.
In God's care we dwell secure.
Teach us your ways, O God,
that we may dwell in your presence.

CALL TO WORSHIP (LUKE 13)

We gather this morning to sing God's praises.
**Blessed is the One who comes
in the name of the Lord!**
We bring our brokenness and seek God's peace.
**Blessed is the One who comes
in the name of the Lord!**
We come to worship the God of love.
**Blessed is the One who comes
in the name of the Lord!**

CONTEMPORARY GATHERING WORDS (GENESIS 15, LUKE 13)

As a mother hen comforts her chicks,
God's love brings us peace!
As stars fill the night sky with heavenly light,
God's blessings fill our lives with joy!

PRAISE SENTENCES (PSALM 27)

The Lord is my light and my salvation.
I am not afraid!

PRAISE SENTENCES (PHILIPPIANS 3)

We are citizens of heaven.
We live with Christ in glory!

PRAISE SENTENCES (GENESIS 15)

God's promises are true.
God's covenant lasts forever!

OPENING PRAYER (PSALM 27, PHILIPPIANS 3)

Faithful God,
we gather as your people,
longing for your presence.
We bring our doubts and fears,

trusting that your grace
will bring us the peace we lack.
May we dwell in your house,
delighting in your beauty.
Teach us your ways,
that we may abide in your grace
and count heaven as our home. Amen.

OPENING PRAYER (PSALM 27)

Eternal God,
we come this morning,
seeking your loving presence.
You alone are completely faithful.
You keep us from evil.
Show us your goodness
and teach us your ways.
May we dwell with you forever,
singing songs of everlasting joy. Amen.

UNISON PRAYER (GENESIS 15, PSALM 27, LUKE 13)

God of the starry night,
your love is as vast
as the night sky.
God of the mother hen,
your love surrounds us
like a warm, downy wing.
Your promise sustains us.
When we are afraid,
your faithfulness sustains us,
and renews our courage.
When evil draws near,
you hide us in your love
and keep us from danger.
Give us grateful hearts and joyous spirits,
that we may live in your presence
and trust in your word. Amen.

PRAYER OF CONFESSION (GENESIS 15, LUKE 13)
O God of all creation,
    your promises are vast,
        yet we fail to trust your word.
We doubt your power
    to transform our lives.
Give us the patience to wait
    for your time,
    for your blessings,
    and for your will to be done.
Help us feel your loving compassion,
    that we may dwell securely
        beneath the wings of your love.
Amen.

WORDS OF ASSURANCE
God's promises are true.
God's love is never-ending.
God protects us from all danger
    and comforts us with love.

PRAYER OF CONFESSION (LUKE 13, PHILIPPIANS 3)
Merciful God,
    we are like lost chicks
        running away from your loving presence.
We fail to trust your promises.
We fear the dangers of this world.
We lack the courage to fight injustice.
We live as enemies of one another,
    rather than as sisters and brothers in Christ.
Forgive us, we pray, and keep us safe.
Give us courage to walk into the future
    with confidence. Amen.

WORDS OF ASSURANCE
Jesus Christ will transform our humiliation into glory.
Stand firm in the Lord.

BENEDICTION (LUKE 13)

May the compassionate love
  of our Lord Jesus Christ
    draw you close,
    keep you safe,
    and bring you peace.

BENEDICTION (GENESIS 15, PHILIPPIANS 3)

Stand firm in the Lord.
Trust in God's promises.
Dwell in the presence of the Almighty.
May the blessings of God's peace
  bring you courage.

BENEDICTION (LUKE 13)

May God give you courage to go forth and say:
  Blessed is the One who comes
  in the name of the Lord!
May God give you hope for tomorrow, when all shall say:
  Blessed is the One who comes
  in the name of the Lord!

MARCH 11, 2007
Third Sunday in Lent
Erik J. Alsgaard

COLOR
Purple

SCRIPTURE READINGS
Isaiah 55:1-9; Psalm 63:1-8; 1 Corinthians 10:1-13; Luke 13:1-9

THEME IDEAS
Repentance, a central theme of Lent, cannot be ignored in today's lessons. Jesus' words are clear: repent or perish. Isaiah's words, "Let the wicked forsake their ways," echo Christ's. Paul's writing gives a strong warning from Israel's history to the Corinthians and to us today: "God was not pleased with most of them, and they were struck down." But repentance is not merely a cessation of sin or a halting of that which is not pleasing in God's sight; it is more than that. Repentance also carries the idea of turning around in a new direction, of doing a one-eighty in your life. Isaiah invites us to embrace the abundant life that God offers us.

CALL TO WORSHIP (ISAIAH 55)
Seek the Lord while God is to be found.
Call upon God while God is near!
Repent of unrighteous ways.

It is never too late to turn to God!
Get rid of evil thoughts.
Let us turn to God, that God may have mercy on us!
For God will pardon our sins and cleanse us
of our transgressions.
We will praise God for the new life we have found!
Alleluia!
Alleluia!

CALL TO WORSHIP (PSALM 63)
Lord, you are our God.
We will praise you with joyful lips.
Lord, you are our God.
Our souls thirst for you.
Lord, you are our God.
We behold your power and majesty.
Lord, you are our God.
We will bless you all of the days of our lives.

CONTEMPORARY GATHERING WORDS (PSALM 63)
O God, you are our God.
We will ever praise you!

PRAISE SENTENCES
New every morning is your mercy, O God.
You save us from our transgressions.
You bless us with steadfast love and mercy.
In true repentance, we find new life.

OPENING PRAYER (LUKE 13)
Gracious and eternal God,
    you call us into a new way of being,
    and give us so many second chances in life.
May your love wash over us,
    as we turn toward you
        from our sinful ways.

Mold us as your people
in new and powerful ways,
that we may be true disciples
of your Son, Jesus Christ,
in whose name we pray. Amen.

OPENING PRAYER (PSALM 63)

Gentle and loving God,
our souls cling to you
like a newborn baby
clings to its mother.
Give us this day the Bread of life,
that as we feast at your table,
our souls may be filled with your praise,
in Jesus' name. Amen.

PRAYER OF CONFESSION

A broken and contrite heart
is the acceptable sacrifice to you, O God.
And so we come before you today,
as sinners in need of your mercy.
Grant us your forgiveness, O God.
Help us turn from our old ways.
Lead us into newness of life,
that our actions may be found pleasing
in your sight. Amen.

UNISON PRAYER

I am no longer my own, but yours. Put me to what you
will, rank me with whom you will; put me to doing, put
me to suffering; let me be employed for you or laid aside
for you, exalted for you or brought low for you; let me be
full, let me be empty, let me have all things, let me have
nothing; I freely and wholeheartedly yield all things to
your pleasure and disposal. And now, glorious and
blessed God, Father, Son, and Holy Spirit, you are mine

and I am yours. So be it. And the covenant made on earth, let it be ratified in heaven. Amen.

BENEDICTION

Turn to the Lord, for God is good.
We have found new life in Christ!
Repent of your sins and find God's forgiveness.
We have found new life in Christ!
Go forth as new creatures, able to serve
and quick to love.
We have found new life in Christ!

MARCH 18, 2007

Fourth Sunday in Lent
Mary J. Scifres

COLOR
Purple

SCRIPTURE READINGS
Joshua 5:9-12; Psalm 32; 2 Corinthians 5:16-21; Luke 15:1-3, 11b-32

THEME IDEAS
Forgiveness leaps off the pages of these Scripture readings as we continue our Lenten journey. God finally welcomes the Israelites into the Promised Land, the psalmist lauds the joy of the forgiven, and Paul writes of the new creation we find through Christ's ministry of reconciliation. But the myriad of issues surrounding forgiveness is best seen in Luke's beloved story of the prodigal son. Today's message need not be a simplistic one, for forgiveness is difficult and complex. And yet, the truth of God's love is this: in Christ Jesus, we are forgiven!

CALL TO WORSHIP (2 CORINTHIANS 5, LUKE 15)
Celebrate and rejoice.
We are the forgiven family of God!
Praise God, who loves us so!
Celebrate and rejoice.
We are the beloved children of God!

Rejoice in Christ, who welcomes us home!
Celebrate and rejoice.
We are the renewed people of God!
Praise to the Spirit, who calls us here!

CALL TO WORSHIP (PSALM 32)

Let the faithful come forth and enter the house of God.
Let our prayers rise to the loving ears of God.
For this is our hiding place,
where the One who always loves us is waiting.
May God's love surround us and hold us close.
May our cries be heard and our sins forgiven.
May our hearts be comforted and our joys renewed.
May our worship be a blessing to one and all.
We bring our worship to God.

CALL TO WORSHIP (PSALM 32)

Stone Church
3/18/07

Be glad in God's love! Rejoice in the Spirit!
Shout for joy and sing God's praise!
Happy are we who know of God's love!
Happy are we who know of Christ's grace!
Be glad in God's love! Rejoice in the Spirit!
Shout for joy and sing God's praise!

CONTEMPORARY GATHERING WORDS (2 CORINTHIANS 5; LUKE 15)

Do you not know? Have you not heard?
In Christ, you are a new creation.
Yes, you! Not someone else—you!
For you, for me, for every person here,
    Christ has blotted out our sins,
    redeemed us through God's love and grace,
    and made us new people.
Welcome, newborn babes!
Christ has given us life
    and welcomes us home!

CONTEMPORARY GATHERING WORDS (LUKE 15)

Let us worship and celebrate!
Many here were lost,
but are now found.
Many here were once far away,
but have been brought near by Christ Jesus.
Many here were once dead,
but are alive again through God's love!
Let us worship and celebrate indeed!

PRAISE SENTENCES (LUKE 15)

Celebrate Jesus! Celebrate!
Celebrate Jesus! Celebrate!

PRAISE SENTENCES (LUKE 15)

Rejoice in God! Rejoice today!
Rejoice in God! Rejoice today!

OPENING PRAYER (JOSHUA 5, 2 CORINTHIANS 5, LUKE 15)

God of forgiveness and grace,
thank you for welcoming us
so warmly and lovingly.
Open our hearts,
that we may fully receive
your grace and love.
Bless us and renew us,
that we may live as the new creations
you envision us to be.
Inspire us to be your kingdom on this earth,
that we may be your promised land
with words that soothe like honey
and actions that nourish like milk. Amen.

OPENING PRAYER (PSALM 32, 2 CORINTHIANS 5)

God of grace and God of glory,
   we pour our prayers
      upon you this day.
Out of our hiding places,
   we have come
      to enter into your glory
         and your grace.
Hold back the rushing waters of life,
   that we may be nourished
      by the life-giving spring of your love.
Cover our sins with your forgiveness,
   that we may walk forth
      as newly inspired children
         of your grace.
Shelter us from the troubles of this world,
   if only for this hour,
      that we might feel
         your protective power.
And surround us with your hope and promise,
   that we might go forth
      blessed by your abundant love and grace.
Amen.

PRAYER OF CONFESSION (PSALM 32, LUKE 15)

Loving Father, Gentle Mother,
   hold us in the arms
      of your forgiveness and grace.
When we run from you
   or abandon your guiding light,
      welcome us back with mercy.
When we squander your gifts
   or reject your generosity,
      love us into right living.
When we hide from our shame
   or mask our guilt,

coax us into the light
of your abundant love.
Hear our prayers, dear Lord.
Be our hiding place of hope and joy,
that we might say with the psalmist,
"Happy are those who are forgiven!"
Amen.

WORDS OF ASSURANCE (PSALM 32, 2 CORINTHIANS 5)
Happy are those who are forgiven.
In Christ Jesus, we are made new again!
Happy are those who are forgiven.
In the name of Jesus Christ, we are forgiven!

BENEDICTION (2 CORINTHIANS 5)
Go forth as ambassadors of Christ.
In Christ, we are made new!
Go forth as beloved children of God.
In Christ, we are forgiven!

BENEDICTION (LUKE 15)
We, who were once lost,
have been found.
We, who were once dead,
have been given new life.
Go into the world,
rejoicing that God has welcomed us home,
and sends us into the world
to share that welcome with all!

MARCH 25, 2007

Fifth Sunday in Lent
Joanne Carlson Brown

COLOR

Purple

SCRIPTURE READINGS

Isaiah 43:16-21; Psalm 126; Philippians 3:4*b*-14; John 12:1-8

THEME IDEAS

As we journey through Lent, we focus on the promises of forgiveness, new life, and extravagant love. As the world begins to bud in spring (in the northern hemisphere), we see Isaiah proclaiming all things new and the former things forgotten. The psalmist comforts those who mourn with the promise of restoration and joy, and with the great things God has done for us. Paul urges us to forget what lies behind and strain forward to what lies ahead. And John's story is about extravagant love in the face of opposition. While in Lent we reflect on what we have done, let these passages move us ahead to new life and new hope and new beginnings, free from the pull and drag of the past.

CALL TO WORSHIP (PSALM 126)

Come, people of God, come into God's presence.
We come with anticipation and longing.
Come, all you who are weeping.

We shall return home with shouts of joy.
Come, all who dream.
We come with laughter and delight.
Come, let us worship our God, who has done great things
for us.

CALL TO WORSHIP (PSALM 126, JOHN 12)
Listen: the heart of God calls to us.
Come, my beloved, my chosen; come home to me.
Let us respond to the invitation with joy and laughter.
Let us bring our dreams and hopes, our jars of ointment,
our longings, our desires, and our love.
Let us be open to the indwelling of God,
who makes all things new.
We come, O God; we come.

CONTEMPORARY GATHERING WORDS (ISAIAH 43)
Look around. What do you see?
All around us, there are signs of new life.
Do not remember the former things.
God is doing a new thing.
Let us worship the God of renewal.

PRAISE SENTENCES (PSALM 126)
God has done great things for us!
Rejoice!
God has restored our fortunes!
Rejoice!
God is doing a new thing!
Rejoice!
God loves us with an extravagant love!
Rejoice!

OPENING PRAYER (ISAIAH 43, PSALM 126)
O God of hopes and dreams,
we come this morning,

longing to put the past behind us
and embrace the new life you bring.
In this time of worship,
may your renewing spirit
fall upon us as water in the desert.
May we be able to hear
the joy of your promises,
and laugh with delight
as we feel your love wash over us,
making us new and whole again.
May we claim our identity
as your chosen people,
your faithful ones,
your beloved disciples. Amen.

OPENING PRAYER

God of extravagant love,
sometimes it is too overwhelming,
too wonderful to grasp—
this love of yours.
As we worship this morning,
open our souls wide—
that every word spoken,
and every note sung
will form and reform
us as your people.
As we drink in your abundant love,
enable us to be conduits
of this gracious love
to all the world. Amen.

PRAYER OF CONFESSION (ISAIAH 43, PSALM 126)

O God of laughter and tears,
we come in this Lenten season
weighed down by the past.
Sometimes we feel trapped
by past actions, past attitudes, past beliefs.

We feel as if we are wandering in a desert,
    carrying burdens, losing our way.
Sometimes we hold fast to this past,
    hold fast to our prejudices and our fears.
We criticize, we judge, we despair,
    we doubt our ability to change.
Break open our hearts,
    pour in your transforming
    and renewing love.
Keep our eyes on the prize—
    new life in you. Amen.

WORDS OF ASSURANCE (ISAIAH 43, PSALM 126)
Do not remember the former things,
    or consider the things of old.
I am about to do a new thing.
Know you are my chosen ones, my beloved.
Come home, forgiven and made new.

BENEDICTION (ISAIAH 43, PSALM 126)
Go forth with tears turned into joy,
weeping transformed into laughter.
We go forth as a renewed people,
with dreams of love and justice for all.
Go forth to claim your identity
as beloved people of God.
God has done great things for us.
We go to spread this good news
to a parched and weary world.

BENEDICTION
Chosen and beloved of God,
    go forth to pour out God's extravagant love
        on all you meet.
Keep your eyes on the prize—
    the call of God to new life in Christ.
Go out rejoicing and declaring God's praise.

APRIL 1, 2007

Palm/Passion Sunday
Bill Hoppe

COLOR
Purple

PALM SUNDAY READINGS
Psalm 118:1-2, 19-29; Luke 19:28-40

PASSION SUNDAY READINGS
Isaiah 50:4-9a; Psalm 31:9-16; Philippians 2:5-11; Luke 22:14–23:56 (or Luke 23:1-49)

THEME IDEAS
The king who is welcomed to Jerusalem with shouts of praise and adulation will die horribly on a cross just a few days later. If we start with Palm Sunday and end with Good Friday, it is easy to view the events of Holy Week as a journey from triumph to tragedy. Instead, the opposite holds true. The triumph is in the tragedy itself, as Paul reminds us in the Philippians passage: Jesus "humbled himself and became obedient to the point of death— / even death on a cross. / Therefore God also highly exalted him / and gave him the name that is above every name." Today, we take this same journey with Jesus, moving from delirious joy to abject sorrow, knowing that our tears will soon turn to surprised laughter. The best is yet to come.

CALL TO WORSHIP (LUKE 19)

Sing glory to God in the highest heaven!
The King is coming!
Even if we keep silent,
the rocks will shout it out!
The King is coming!
The King is coming!
**Blessed is the One who comes
in the name of the Lord!**

CALL TO WORSHIP (PSALM 118)

Give thanks to God. The Lord is good.
God's steadfast love endures forever.
Declare it with thanksgiving.
God's steadfast love endures forever.
The Lord is my salvation.
God has become my deliverer.
The Lord is God!
The Lord has given us light!
Give thanks to God. The Lord is good.
God's steadfast love endures forever.

CONTEMPORARY GATHERING WORDS (LUKE 19)

A borrowed colt is loosed.
Our Master needs it!
He rides over a carpet of cloaks.
Hosanna to the King!
He rides in humble majesty.
The rocks cry out!
Shout for joy!
Hosanna to the King!

CONTEMPORARY GATHERING WORDS (ISAIAH 50)

God helps me. I know that I won't be shamed.
The One who will clear my name is at my side.
God vindicates me. The Lord is near!

Where are my enemies? Who argues against me?
The Lord stands by me. Who can dispute my cause?

PRAISE SENTENCES (LUKE 19)
Our King has come,
riding on a donkey.
The king is here.
Shout for joy!
Our Savior has come
amid waving palms and cheers of praise.
The savior is here.
Shout alleluia!
Jesus has come,
riding on a donkey.
Jesus is here.
Shout hosanna!
Blessed is the One who comes
in the name of the Lord!
(*B. J. Beu*)

OPENING PRAYER (LUKE 22, LUKE 23, ISAIAH 50)
We welcome you, Lord Jesus.
Hosanna to our king!
The greatest among us has become the least.
Hosanna to our servant king!
Gracious master, humble teacher,
with a word, you sustain our weary souls.
We stand with you in this time of trial.
We stand with you, though you have done no wrong.
Remember us, Lord Jesus. Remember us!
Remember us when you come into your kingdom!
Blessed is the One who comes in the name of the Lord!
Hosanna in the highest! Amen.

OPENING PRAYER OR INVITATION TO COMMUNION (LUKE 22)
Lord Jesus,
your hour has come.

You arrived as a king
   in the midst of a procession
      of waving palms.
You move among us
   as one who serves—
      an example for us to follow.
How you have longed for us to join you:
   to eat and drink with you
      at your table in your kingdom.
Now your body is broken for us,
   like a loaf of bread.
The cup poured out for us
   is the new covenant sealed by your blood.
We remember your sacrifice.
We can never forget such amazing love.
How we long to join you
   at your table in your kingdom.
In your name we pray, amen.

PRAYER OF CONFESSION (PSALM 31)

Lord, in your mercy,
   hear me.
By your grace,
   help me.
I'm in great trouble.
I can't see or think clearly.
My body wastes away
   from grief and sorrow.
My strength fails me.
The burden of my misery
   is crushing me.
Friends, neighbors, and family avoid me.
All who see me quickly turn away.
Yet even in the depth of my despair, Lord,
   I place my trust in you.
You are my God!

Let your face shine upon me and save me,
in your unfailing and steadfast love! Amen.

WORDS OF ASSURANCE (PSALM 118)

All who call on the name of the Lord are answered.
God's steadfast love endures forever.
God is by your side. There is nothing to be afraid of.
The Lord stands beside you to help.
This is the day that the Lord has made!
Rejoice and be glad.

BENEDICTION (PHILIPPIANS 2, ISAIAH 50)

May the same mind be in you that was in Christ Jesus:
the One who never turned backward in defiance;
the One who gave his back to the lash;
the One who faced spitting and insult.
May your bearing be that of Christ Jesus:
the One who emptied himself;
the One who took the form of a servant;
the One who was raised to the heights
and given the name above all names.
May your life declare the lordship of Jesus Christ,
to the glory of God! Amen!

BENEDICTION

On the back of a donkey,
Jesus came to bless us.
With love in his heart,
Jesus came to save us.
From the power of death,
Jesus came to set us free.
Go with the blessings of God's anointed.
(B. J. Beu)

APRIL 5, 2007

Holy Thursday
Sara Dunning Lambert

COLOR
Purple

SCRIPTURE READINGS
Exodus 12:1-4 (5-10) 11-14; Psalm 116:1-4, 12-19;
1 Corinthians 11:23-26; John 13:1-17, 31b-35

THEME IDEAS
Today we focus on the events leading up to the crucifixion and death of Christ. We hear again the familiar stories of the Passover, the Last Supper, and the washing of the disciples' feet by Jesus. Psalm 116, one of the psalms sung during the Passover, reflects these settings with images of the cup of salvation, sacrifice, and God's mercy and protection. We are called to remember and perform the ritual acts that set us apart as Christians. Many congregations celebrate Holy Communion, experience foot washing, or share in a Passover Seder meal. Visual images of the cup and bread, a washbasin and towel, or elements of the Seder meal may be used.

CALL TO WORSHIP (PSALM 116, EXODUS 12)
God of infinite wisdom, we come into your presence
with open arms.
I love the Lord, because God has heard my voice

and my supplications.
As we repeat the ancient stories, we mark our hearts
with the blood of the lamb.
**I love the Lord, because God has heard my voice
and my supplications.**
Bless us with your protection, as we reflect on the cup
of salvation Christ offers us.
**I love the Lord, because God has heard my voice
and my supplications.**
Amen!

CALL TO WORSHIP (1 CORINTHIANS 11, JOHN 13)

Holy One, we come in remembrance of you.
Wash us clean, O Lord.
We seek the cup of the new covenant.
Wash us clean, O Lord.
The bread of forgiveness reminds us of your love.
Wash us clean, O Lord.
Let us join together in praise and thanksgiving.
Wash us clean, O Lord.

CONTEMPORARY GATHERING WORDS

Come to worship with joyful praise!
God is merciful!
Come to the table with thanksgiving!
God is merciful!
Lay down your burdens in peace!
God is merciful!
Feel the cleansing power of Christ!
God is merciful!

PRAISE SENTENCES (EXODUS 12, 1 CORINTHIANS 11)

We are washed clean by the blood of Christ!
Glorify the name of Jesus Christ—
Lamb of God, Servant, and Bread of Life!

We are washed clean by the blood of Christ!
Lift up the cup of salvation,
   and call on the name of the Lord.
We are washed clean by the blood of Christ!

OPENING PRAYER (EXODUS 12, PSALM 116)

Heavenly Lord,
   we faithfully remember your love
      for the people of the Exodus.
In the blood of the Lamb
   we see your awesome emblem of protection,
   made perfect in the sacrifice
      of your Son.
We are connected, through time, faith, and love,
   with your servants of the Passover.
We sing together the psalm of protection
   and thanksgiving for deliverance.
Lead us into these days of reflection
   with a sense of peace, forgiveness, and hope.
Let us experience the forgiveness of the Last Supper
   as we prepare for the despair of Good Friday
      and the promise of the Easter resurrection. Amen.

OPENING PRAYER (1 CORINTHIANS 11, JOHN 13)

May we be your servants, Lord.
Teach us to wash the feet
   of our brothers and sisters
      in faith and love.
With Christ as our example,
   help us follow your new commandment
      to love one another.
May we be known as your disciples:
   at home, at church, and in the world.
Lead us in your ways,
   as we seek the healing power
      of your forgiveness and peace. Amen.

PRAYER OF CONFESSION

Holy One,
 we come to your table expectantly.
Remind us of the healing power
 of your love.
We long to seek your protection
 from our fears and our sins.
But far too often,
 we try to brave our problems alone.
We lay before you our burdens, tattered hopes,
 and shattered dreams.
We remember the terrible sacrifice
 you suffered for us,
 and are humbled by your fierce love—
 your word made flesh, given for us,
 that we might live.
Love us, forgive us,
 and protect us, O God. Amen.

WORDS OF ASSURANCE

Hear these words of assurance.
God loves us so much that we receive new life in Christ.
Remember this each time you eat the bread of life
 and drink from the cup of salvation. Amen.

BENEDICTION (EXODUS 12, PSALM 116)

Awesome God, as we retell the Passover story,
 we ask your blessing on us today.
Pass over our failings and hear our supplications
 as we praise your ever-present love.
We are your servants now and forever. Amen!

BENEDICTION (1 CORINTHIANS 11, JOHN 13)

As the time continues inexorably toward Good Friday,
 we are reminded of God's grace in the Last Supper.
 We remember you, O Lord.

May we be ever mindful of the sacrifice of Christ,
who died for us.
Wash clean our hearts and minds.
Lord of the new commandment,
send us forth in your love.
We are your servants, Lord. Amen!

APRIL 6, 2007

Good Friday
Mark Dowdy

COLOR
Black or None

SCRIPTURE READINGS
Isaiah 52:13–53:12; Psalm 22; Hebrews 10:1-25; John 18:1–19:42

THEME IDEAS
Good Friday. What's that all about? What's good about this day? The day they crucified my Lord! Scholars are divided as to why this day is called "good." Some scholars suggest that the term "Good Friday" arises from John's gospel. As Jesus is lifted up on the cross, both physically and spiritually, Christ is lifted up in glory. Other scholars suggest that "good" is a misprint, and the day should be called "God Friday," the day God wept because of the death of God's child, the day Jesus experienced the ultimate of what all human beings experience. Physical death! This is one more event to let us know that God knows all there is to know about human life—and death.

CALL TO WORSHIP
Our way through Lent has brought us to this hour.
During our journey of forgiveness and restoration,

**we have faced old habits and explored new
possibilities.**
We have felt God's protection.
We have heard about God's plans for our lives.
We have renewed our friendship with God.
**We have experienced God's gifts of silence
and introspection.**
We now experience the passion of Jesus,
who suffered and died this day.
**Let us worship God together,
as we remember the meaning of Jesus' death,
and embrace the new life to come.**

CONTEMPORARY GATHERING WORDS

We have gathered this Good Friday
to remember the betrayal, humiliation,
and crucifixion of Jesus.
We have gathered to experience anew
the events that would change the world.
May we experience all the pathos of that day,
and may we participate in its meaning together.

PRAISE SENTENCES (ISAIAH 52, JOHN 18–19)

Jesus is lifted up on high!
Exalt him!
Jesus draws the world to himself!
Exalt him!
Jesus is lifted up on high!
Exalt him!
(B. J. Beu)

OPENING PRAYER (ISAIAH 52, JOHN 18–19)

Lamb of God,
We hid our faces,
as you were spat upon
and counted as accursed.

We watched silently
    as you were led to the slaughter
        as one who blasphemed against God.
Open our hearts this night (day),
    that we may feel your pain
        and know the cost of our salvation.
Amen.
(B. J. Beu)

OPENING PRAYER (PSALM 22)

O God,
    when our lives ache with pain,
        and we feel alone,
        we long for your presence.
We feel the empty longing
    of the psalmist and of Jesus:
        "My God, my God,
            why do you desert me?
        We cry desperately for help,
            but it does not come."
We feel scorned and abused
    by those closest to us.
Like a pack of dogs,
    evil people close in on us.
They surround us and tear at us.
Stay close to us, O God,
    and we will praise your power
        to all people!
In the midst of the congregation,
    we will praise you. Amen.

PRAYER OF CONFESSION (JOHN 18)

Just as Judas betrayed Jesus out of good intentions,
    thinking he could force Jesus' hand
        against the Romans,
    we too betray Jesus out of good intentions,

thinking he will take our side
and fight for us.
Just as Caiaphas sacrificed Jesus out of good intentions,
believing it better for one man to die for the people,
we too sacrifice others out of good intentions,
convincing ourselves of the justness of our cause,
and that our actions are for the greater good.
Just as Peter denied Jesus three times
when asked if he knew the Nazarene,
we too deny Jesus many times
when strangers ask us about our faith.
Just as Pilate washed his hands of responsibility
of doing what he knew to be right,
we too have condemned the innocent
and let the guilty go free.
Forgive us, kind Jesus, and help us never again
betray or deny you. Amen.

ASSURANCE OF PARDON
Hear the words of Jesus, "Abba, forgive them.
For they do not know what they do."

BENEDICTION
Be filled with the love of Christ
until we gather again to celebrate New Life!
And all God's waiting people say together,
Amen.

APRIL 8, 2007

Easter Sunday

B. J. Beu

COLOR
White

SCRIPTURE READINGS
Acts 10:34-43; Psalm 118:1-2, 14-24; 1 Corinthians 15:19-26; John 20:1-18 (or Luke 24:1-12)

THEME IDEAS
The steadfast love spoken of by the psalmist has raised Jesus from the dead. The healer and miracle worker from Galilee is now judge of the living and the dead. How will we recognize our risen savior? Jesus calls each of us by name—a call to discipleship and service. The hymn "Christ the Lord Is Risen Today" says it all. Everything else is commentary.

CALL TO WORSHIP (PSALM 118)
O give thanks to the Lord, for God is good.
God's steadfast love endures forever!
The Lord is our strength and our might.
God has become our salvation!
The stone that the builders rejected
has become the chief cornerstone.
Christ is risen. Alleluia!

CALL TO WORSHIP (JOHN 20, LUKE 24)

The night is far gone; there is dew on the grass.
We walk with the women to the tomb.
The stone is rolled back; only his grave clothes remain.
We weep with the women, for all hope seems lost.
Angels question our tears, for God is stronger than death.
Jesus calls us by name, and we behold his glory.
Shout it from the mountaintop, Christ is risen! Alleluia!
Christ is risen indeed.

CALL TO WORSHIP OR BENEDICTION (PSALM 118, 1 CORINTHIANS 15)

The stone that the builders rejected
has become the chief cornerstone.
This is the Lord's doing.
It is marvelous in our eyes.
Through the power of Jesus' resurrection,
we are made alive in Christ.
This is the day that the Lord has made.
Let us rejoice and be glad in it.

CONTEMPORARY GATHERING WORDS (ACTS 10, 1 CORINTHIANS 15)

Hear the good news. Christ is risen!
But we watched him die.
Hear the good news. Christ is risen!
But we saw him buried in the tomb.
Hear the good news. Christ is risen!
We will sing with the angels
and laugh with the living God.

CONTEMPORARY GATHERING WORDS

Shout for joy.
Death is cheated.
Clap your hands.

Christ is risen.
Dance and sing.
Jesus reigns with power and might.

PRAISE SENTENCES

The tomb is empty!
Christ is risen!
The women are dancing!
Christ is risen!
Death is defeated!
Christ is risen!

PRAISE SENTENCES (PSALM 118, 1 CORINTHIANS 15)

Give thanks to the Lord!
Our God is stronger than death!
Give thanks to the Lord!
God has raised Jesus from the dead!
Give thanks to the Lord!
God's steadfast love endures forever!
Give thanks to the Lord!

OPENING PRAYER (ACTS 10)

Risen Savior,
 it seems a lifetime
  since you broke bread with us,
  offering your body and blood
   for the forgiveness of our sins;
 it seems an eternity
  since we beheld your broken body,
  hanging lifeless on a cross
   for the salvation of us all.
As we celebrate your resurrection,
 help us remember the ostprice you paid
  for the joy we feel today.
May our lives reflect

the depth of gratitude we feel
as your disciples. Amen.

OPENING PRAYER (PSALM 118, JOHN 20, LUKE 24)
Mighty God,
> your steadfast love endures forever.
As we behold the glory of our salvation,
> take us back to that moment of mystery—
>> when the women first beheld the empty tomb,
>> when hope was mingled with grief and loss.
Before we shout our alleluias,
> remind us of the moment
>> when the disciples' despair
>>> was transported into glimpses
>>> of new possibilities.
Help us treasure the raw power of Easter,
> that we may never take our salvation for granted.
Amen.

BENEDICTION (ACTS 10, 1 CORINTHIANS 15)
God, who raised Jesus from the dead,
offers us life and the forgiveness of our sins.
> **We rejoice in Christ our Savior**
> **whose resurrection brings us life!**
Go forth with God's blessings.
> **We go forth, blessed by the living God.**

APRIL 15, 2007

Second Sunday of Easter
Jamie Greening

COLOR
White

SCRIPTURE READINGS
Acts 5:27-32; Psalm 150; Revelation 1:4-8; John 20:19-31

THEME IDEAS
Easter's joy continues this week, as we emphasize resurrection, rebirth, life, and renewal. The atoning work of the pierced and crucified Jesus is prominent in the passages from Acts and Revelation. Forgiveness and peace are reoccurring themes, and these can be linked together as cause and effect. Springtime offers illustrations and ideas for drawing parallels between spiritual renewal and seasonal renewal. The lesson from Revelation emphasizes the Alpha and the Omega as the beginning and the end. If Easter is the beginning (alpha) of eternal life, then the abiding presence of Jesus is the completion (omega) in the life of the believer.

CALL TO WORSHIP (PSALM 150)
Praise the Lord!
God has defeated death.
Praise the Lord!
Sing the Easter song.

Praise the Lord!
Breathe the air of life.
Alleluia.

CALL TO WORSHIP (REVELATION 1)

To the church from the Alpha and Omega:
Peace and grace.
To the church from the Pierced One:
Freedom.
To the church from the Firstborn of the Dead:
Life.

CONTEMPORARY GATHERING WORDS (JOHN 20)

It is the first day of the week.
God Almighty is with us.
Peace be with us.
It is the first day of the week.
Jesus is here.
Peace be with us.
It is the first day of the week.
The Holy Spirit is upon us.
Peace be with us.

PRAISE SENTENCES (ACTS 5)

The God of our ancestors raised Jesus from the dead!
Jesus is exalted to the right hand of God.
We are witnesses of God's forgiveness.

PRAISE SENTENCES (PSALM 150)

Praise God in this sanctuary.
Praise God for salvation in days gone by.
Praise God for salvation here today.
Praise God's surpassing greatness with music.
Bless God's holy name with life and breath.

OPENING PRAYER (JOHN 20)

Our Lord and our God,
  like doubting Thomas so long ago,
  it is sometimes difficult for us to believe
  in new life and Resurrection.
We ask you to turn our doubts
  into vibrant faith.
We have not seen,
  but help us believe. Amen.

OPENING PRAYER

Jesus, you are alive!
Breathe life into us this day.
Grant us enthusiasm.
Grant us joy.
Grant us rebirth.
Help us be alive!
Amen.

UNISON PRAYER (REVELATION 1)

To the One who loves us,
  be glory and power.
To the One who has freed us from our sins,
  be glory and power.
To the One who has brought us into the kingdom,
  be glory and power.
Look, the One long-awaited is coming.
Amen.

BENEDICTION (ACTS 5)

We are witnesses of marvelous things.
  The Holy Spirit works within us.
Let us leave this place to tell what we have seen.
  Christ is risen.
Christ is risen indeed!

BENEDICTION (JOHN 20)

We have heard the good news that we might believe.
We believe Jesus is the Christ.
We have life in Jesus' name.
We go out to proclaim what God has done.

APRIL 22, 2007

Third Sunday of Easter
Mary J. Scifres

COLOR
White

SCRIPTURE READINGS
Acts 9:1-6 (7-20); Psalm 30; Revelation 5:11-14; John 21:1-19

THEME IDEAS
Hope and new life emerge on this Sunday in the Easter season, inspiring and challenging us to share Christ's message of hope and love with a world in need. Let the scales fall from our eyes as courage moves us into ministry. With Peter, may we say, "Yes, Lord; you know that I love you." Christ calls us, as Christ called both Peter and Paul, to tend God's flocks throughout the world.

CALL TO WORSHIP (JOHN 21)
Christ is calling:
"Do you love me?"
Christ is hoping:
"Do you love me?"
Christ is trusting:
"Do you love me?"
We have come to answer:
"Yes, we love you!"

We have come with hope:
"Yes, we love you!"
We have come with trust:
"Yes, we love you!"
Let us hear Christ's words, sense God's presence,
and receive the Spirit's nurture.
God calls us to feed Christ's sheep,
and tend the flocks of God's world.

CALL TO WORSHIP (PSALM 30)

Exalt the Lord, our God, who restores our lives.
Praise the God of love, who lifts us from despair.
Rejoice, for day has dawned. Christ is risen indeed!
Sing a song of joy, for Christ has called us
to the dance!

CALL TO WORSHIP (REVELATION 5)

Worthy is the One who calls us now to pray.
Worthy is our God, who lives within our lives.
Blessed is the One who rose from death's strong bonds.
Blessed is the One whose Spirit gives us strength.
Glory be to God, glory to God on high.
Glory to the Lamb, the Risen Christ of life!

CONTEMPORARY GATHERING WORDS (JOHN 21)

Do we really love Christ?
Are we living our love?
Do we feed the world?
Do we care for the lambs?
Question upon question....
Challenge upon challenge....
Let us question together.
Let us worship our God,
and find the strength
to face the challenge
of following Christ!

PRAISE SENTENCES (REVELATION 5)

Blessing and honor and glory to our God!
Blessing and honor and glory to our God!

OPENING PRAYER (PSALM 30)

God of the dance and of our lives,
    we come to you this day,
    inviting you to lead our dance.
Let your wisdom guide our steps,
    your hope fill our songs.
Let your joy fill our days,
    your resurrection restore our lives.
Establish us as your people,
    strong and sure in our steps.
Inspire us for works of love,
    filled with joy and laughter.
In thanks and praise, we pray. Amen.

OPENING PRAYER (ACTS 9)

Amazing God,
    speak to us in clarity and power,
    as you once descended
      and spoke to Paul.
Clear the cloudiness of our vision,
    and open our ears to receive your word.
As we receive your Spirit,
    grant us courage to answer "Yes!"
    and send us forth to serve your world.

OPENING PRAYER (JOHN 21)

Holy and loving God,
    we come to you
      as both sheep
      and shepherds.
We yearn for your care,
    your loving touch.

But we also yearn to be useful—
　　to care for those who are hurting,
　　and to ease the burden
　　　　of those who are troubled
　　　　　　and plagued by sorrow.
Strengthen our resolve,
　　and grant us the courage
　　　　to hear your call,
　　　　receive your care,
　　　　and share your love
　　　　　　with a world in need. Amen.

BENEDICTION (REVELATION 5)

And now, to the One who sits upon God's throne:
blessing and honor and glory forevermore.
Blessing and honor and glory forevermore!

BENEDICTION (PSALM 30)

God has turned our sorrow to joy,
our mourning into dancing!
Christ has given us life anew,
calling us into the light.
May the Spirit lead us on.
May Christ dance in our hearts
and in our lives.
Amen and amen!

BENEDICTION (JOHN 21)

We have been called, as lovers of God,
to tend Christ's lambs,
and to feed God's sheep.
Go forth as shepherds of love.
The Shepherd of Love leads us forth.

APRIL 29, 2007

Fourth Sunday of Easter
Laura Jaquith Bartlett

COLOR
White

SCRIPTURE READINGS
Acts 9:36-43; Psalm 23; Revelation 7:9-17; John 10:22-30

THEME IDEAS
One might think that a postmodern, urban society such as ours might struggle with the many shepherd images in today's readings. But the radical comfort offered still comes across in a compelling way. To be able to give ourselves completely to one who nurtures, protects, provides, and heals is incredibly inviting. And clearly, this is no ordinary shepherd. This shepherd offers eternal life, a vision that is painted in elaborate detail in the Revelation text.

CALL TO WORSHIP (PSALM 23, REVELATION 7, JOHN 10)
(If possible, use three different voices as leaders.)
Hear words of comfort:
My sheep hear my voice, and they follow me.
The Lord is my shepherd, I shall not want.

God will wipe away every tear from their eyes.
**Surely goodness and mercy shall follow me
all the days of my life.**
I give them eternal life, and they will never perish.
**I shall dwell in the house of the Lord
my whole life long.**

CONTEMPORARY GATHERING WORDS

Get up! Get up!
It is too early in the morning to be energetic.
(Alternate: It's too late in the day to be energetic.)
Wake up to the possibilities of God's surprises!
We are not sure we can break out of our old ruts.
Arise and open your hearts to the resurrection!
We are an Easter people! Praise God for new life!

CONTEMPORARY GATHERING WORDS
(PSALM 23, JOHN 10)

Come! Walk with the One who is our shepherd.
God is our guide and our protector.
Come! Follow the One who leads us into salvation.
God is our guide and our protector.
Come! Worship the One who offers us eternal life.
God is our guide and our protector.

PRAISE SENTENCES (REVELATION 7)

Blessing and glory and wisdom and thanksgiving
and honor and power and might be to our God
forever and ever!
Amen!

PRAISE SENTENCES (PSALM 23, REVELATION 7)

Salvation belongs to our God!
The Lord is our Shepherd,
the One who provides a feast.
We will never hunger again.

God guides us to springs of the water of life.
We will never thirst again.
Come into God's presence.
God wipes away our tears.

OPENING PRAYER (PSALM 23, REVELATION 7, JOHN 10)

Shepherd God,
   our needs bring us to your pasture.
We come with our fears and doubts,
   and you promise to protect us from evil.
We come with our hunger and thirst,
   and you offer us a banquet that never ends.
We come with our hurts and wounds,
   and you anoint us with healing.
We come with our grief and sadness,
   and you wipe away our tears.
God, we thank you for your care,
   for your guidance, and for your love.
As we worship you this day,
   our hearts sing with the joy
      of being in your presence,
      all the days of our lives. Amen.

PRAYER OF CONFESSION

O God,
   we have heard the Easter story over and over,
   yet we still find ourselves skeptical
      of tales of resurrection.
We long to believe in the offer of eternal life,
   but we continue to cling to old fears.
Give us new eyes to see your promises.
Open our hearts
   to the possibilities
      of new life within us.
Help us break out of old patterns

of doubt and disbelief,
that we might be resurrected
to your vision of love and mercy. Amen.

WORDS OF ASSURANCE (PSALM 23, REVELATION 7)

The God who leads you, guides you, and comforts you
will never desert you.
God will wipe away your tears, and restore your soul.
Thanks be to God!

PRAYER OF THANKSGIVING (PSALM 23)

God of abundance,
you lead us into green pastures
and protect us from evil.
Our cup overflows with your blessings.
In gratitude, we offer you all we have,
knowing that you are the source
of all good gifts.
Take our gifts, take our service,
take our very lives, and use them,
that others might know
the goodness and mercy
you offer freely. Amen.

BENEDICTION (PSALM 23, REVELATION 7, JOHN 10)

As you leave this place,
remember that God wipes away every tear;
remember that Christ leads you as a shepherd;
remember that the Holy Spirit empowers you
with the possibilities of new life. Amen.

BENEDICTION

Blessing and glory be to our God.
Amen!

Wisdom and thanksgiving be to our God.
Amen!
Honor and power and might be to our God
forever and ever.
Amen! Alleluia!

MAY 6, 2007

Fifth Sunday of Easter
Robert Blezard

COLOR
White

SCRIPTURE READINGS
Acts 11:1-18; Psalm 148; Revelation 21:1-6; John 13:31-35

THEME IDEAS
Today's readings reinforce the Easter message of God's radical salvation. The Acts passage tells us that through Christ, God has done a new thing—brought reconciliation to all peoples of the earth, not just the chosen people of Israel. The Revelation passage reveals the prophecy that Jesus brings a new creation—a new heaven and a new earth—and new lives for all of us as well. And the passage from John tells us that our new lives, and our relationships in this new life, will be under the command to love.

CALL TO WORSHIP (ACTS 11)
Come, hear the Message!
God has come to save us.
God brings reconciliation.
Our families, communities, and nations will be saved.
God loves and redeems the world.
God has come to save us.

CALL TO WORSHIP (REVELATION 21)

Let us gather, we who are thirsty!
God gives us water to drink as a gift
from the spring of the water of life.
Let us gather, we who are downcast.
God will wipe every tear from our eyes.
Let us gather, we who grieve.
Mourning and crying and pain will be no more.
Let us gather, we who desire new life.
God is making all things new.
Death will be no more.

CONTEMPORARY GATHERING WORDS (REVELATION 21)

In our busy "24/7" lives,
where is God when we are stressed out,
overwhelmed, and discouraged?
How many of us have wondered that?
(Raise your hand to invite responses.)
We sometimes think of God as a distant deity,
sitting on a satin cushion in a dreamy, faraway heaven,
but the Bible tells us otherwise.
God is here. God is near.
Like a good Mom,
God will wipe away our every tear
and hold the tissue as we blow our noses.
Like a good Dad,
God gets up when we call out at night
and lets us drink from the spring of the water of life.
God is here. God is near.
Thanks be to God.

PRAISE SENTENCES (PSALM 148)

Twinkling stars, wandering planets, shooting comets,
they all praise their maker. We, too, praise God!
Rushing rivers, mighty oceans, morning dew,

they all praise their maker. **We, too, praise God!**
Dainty hummingbirds, howling wolves, skittish squirrels,
they all praise their maker. We, too, praise God!
Gurgling babies, defiant youth, sighing elderly,
they all praise their maker. We, too, praise God!
Wistful winds, sturdy forests, unmoved mountains,
they all praise their maker. We, too, praise God!

OPENING PRAYER (REVELATION 21)

Eternal and gracious God,
    source of all goodness,
        we gather in your house to worship you,
            and to praise your holy name.
Born into darkness and confusion,
    we are drawn to your light
        and the dawn of your glory.
Open our hearts, inspire our minds,
    and infuse our souls
        with your presence. Amen.

OPENING PRAYER (ACTS 11)

Holy God,
    with love for the whole human family,
    you wash the stain of sin from our souls
        with ordinary water
        and your divine Spirit.
Let that Holy Spirit fall upon us today,
    to guide us, to inflame our imagination,
    and to tantalize us with visions
        of what is to come. Amen.

PRAYER OF CONFESSION (JOHN 13)

Merciful God,
    your Son gave us a new commandment:
        love one another.

We confess that, again and again,
  we have broken that commandment:
    through our selfish love for wealth
      that blinds us to the sight of your poor;
    through our obsessive desire for security
      that deafens us to the cries of those
        who live daily with violence and oppression;
    through our silence in the face of injustice
      that leaves us feeling powerless and ashamed.
Help us show everyone
  that we are disciples of Jesus Christ
  by how much we love. Amen.

WORDS OF ASSURANCE (REVELATION 21)

God, the Alpha and the Omega,
  the beginning and the end,
  makes all things new.
May God's Spirit
  dry your tears of shame and sorrow,
  and bring you to new lives
  of love and service.

BENEDICTION (ACTS 11)

May God, who created you,
  continue to bring newness to your life.
May Jesus, who redeemed you,
  give you the repentance that leads to life.
And may the Holy Spirit, who sustains you,
  work within you and show you God's truth.

BENEDICTION (JOHN 13)

Jesus gave us a new commandment—
  that we love one another.
Go forth to serve God
  and love your brothers and sisters
  as Christ has loved us.

MAY 13, 2007

Sixth Sunday of Easter
Festival of the Christian
Home/Mother's Day
Mary Petrina Boyd

COLOR
White

SCRIPTURE READINGS
Acts 16:9-15; Psalm 67; Revelation 21:1-10, 22–22:5; John 14:23-29

THEME IDEAS
God's people gather by the river. In Philippi, they gathered to spread the gospel to Lydia and the other women. At the end of time, the faithful will gather by the glory of the river of life under the abundant fruits of the tree of life. Between these events, Jesus promises a deep and abiding peace to those who love him. And he promises to return.

CALL TO WORSHIP (PSALM 67)
Lord, you have come to save all people.
Let the peoples praise you, O God.
Let all the peoples praise you.
You bring justice to the earth.

Let the peoples praise you, O God.
Let all the peoples praise you.
You bless the land with abundance.
Let the peoples praise you, O God.
Let all the peoples praise you.

CALL TO WORSHIP (REVELATION 22, PSALM 67, JOHN 14)

Shall we gather at the river?
We gather to drink from the waters of life.
Shall we gather at the river?
We gather to feast on your words of truth.
Shall we gather at the river?
We gather to find your peace.
Shall we gather at the river?
We gather to praise you as we gather to worship.

CALL TO WORSHIP OR CONTEMPORARY GATHERING WORDS (REVELATION 21)

God is here.
God dwells with us.
We are the people of God.
God is with us.
God is the Alpha and the Omega.
God is the beginning and the end.
God loves and cares for us.
We are God's children.

CONTEMPORARY GATHERING WORDS (ACTS 16, REVELATION 22)

Come to the river.
Hear the word of God.
Come to the river.
See the tree of life.
Come to the river.
Worship the Lord of heaven and earth.

PRAISE SENTENCES (REVELATION 21)

See, the home of God is among mortals.
God will dwell with us, and we will be God's people.
Death will be no more;
mourning and pain will be no more.
Rejoice in the newness of God's love!

PRAISE SENTENCES (JOHN 14)

We have nothing to fear.
Jesus gives us peace.

OPENING PRAYER (ACTS 16, JOHN 14, REVELATION 22)

We come to you, O God,
    drawn by the power of your love.
We come to hear your good news.
We come to find new life.
We come to satisfy our thirst
    for your holy word.
We come to feed our hunger
    for your love.
Satisfy our desire for you,
    and give us your peace,
    that we may be a blessing to others. Amen.

OPENING PRAYER (ACTS 16)

We gather together,
    longing for your word, O God.
Open our hearts,
    that we may hear
        what you would say to us this day.
Lead us to believe
    in the power of your love.
Help us offer one another
    the gracious hospitality
        of your grace. Amen.

UNISON PRAYER (FESTIVAL OF THE CHRISTIAN HOME, MOTHER'S DAY)

Compassionate God,
    with a mother's love
        you care for us.
In your arms,
    we find peace
        in uncertain times.
You feed us
    with the fruits of compassion,
    and give us the waters of life
        to sustain us.
You set us in families
    in which to grow
        and learn your word.
You give us children to teach.
In your household
    we find a deep peace,
    and the companionship
        of the faithful.
Turn our hearts to you, O God,
    that we may share your love
        with all your family. Amen.

PRAYER OF CONFESSION (FESTIVAL OF THE CHRISTIAN HOME/MOTHER'S DAY)

Lord God,
    we pray for our families.
Strengthen us in your love.
Forgive our failures:
    we let bitterness destroy love;
    we let jealousy and resentment
        keep us separated from one another;
    we let old hurts divide us;
    we fail to care for our children
        with your life-giving love;

we resent our responsibilities
    to care for one another.
Give us the courage
    to reach out to one another with love.
Give us the wisdom
    to see your face
        reflected in those around us.
Give us the strength
    to forgive one another.
Help us be your faithful children. Amen.

WORDS OF ASSURANCE
God is with us.
God brings us peace.

BENEDICTION (PSALM 67, JOHN 14)
May God be gracious to us.
We go with God's blessings.
May God's face shine upon us.
We go with God's peace.

BENEDICTION (JOHN 14)
Jesus said, "Peace I leave with you;
    my peace I give to you.
I do not give to you as the world gives.
Do not let your hearts be troubled,
    and do not let them be afraid."
May the peace of Christ
    make you fearless
        as you spread the good news
           of God's love.

MAY 20, 2007

Ascension Sunday

Jamie Greening

COLOR
White

SCRIPTURE READINGS
Acts 1:1-11; Psalm 47; Ephesians 1:15-23; Luke 24:44-53

THEME IDEAS
Textually and liturgically, the main theme is the ascension of Jesus Christ. The ascension and lordship of Christ illustrate various doctrinal concepts of power, victory, dominion, and glory—themes conveyed in the christological title *Christus Victor*. Additionally, Christ's parting words to spread the gospel provide an excellent context to focus on missions. The Ephesians passage opens a window to discuss the church and its inevitable victory because of Christ's victory. Luke's gospel can be explicated to show that Christ is the promised One foretold by Moses, the prophets, and the psalmists.

CALL TO WORSHIP (PSALM 47)
Clap your hands, all you nations.
We clap our hands to God.
Shout to the heavens with cries of joy.
We shout with all our heart. Alleluia!
How awesome is the Lord most high!

CALL TO WORSHIP (LUKE 24)

We have gathered to hear the law.
For it tells of Jesus.
We have gathered to study the prophets.
For they tell of Jesus.
We have gathered around the Scriptures.
For they tell of the Christ.
We are witnesses of these things.
Let us worship with joy.

CONTEMPORARY GATHERING WORDS (PSALM 47, LUKE 24, ACTS 1)

Jesus blessed us and went to heaven,
telling us to wait for the Holy Spirit.
Christ has ascended.
Jesus is Lord over all the nations.
Christ is enthroned in power.
In this, our Jerusalem, we await the Spirit's descent.

PRAISE SENTENCES (EPHESIANS 1)

God raised Jesus from the dead.
Jesus reigns with God in the heavens.
All things are under God's control.
Jesus is the head of the church.
We gather to sing God's praises.

OPENING PRAYER

Lord Jesus,
you have taken your place
at the right hand of God,
the Father Almighty.
You have ascended to Mt. Zion.
We await the illumination
and guidance of your Holy Spirit. Amen.

OPENING PRAYER

Our Savior Jesus Christ,
you have ascended on high.

Pull us upward
   to focus on the things that are above.
Pull us upward
   to think of the noble and the beautiful.
Pull us upward
   to the worthy pursuit of ministry.
Pull us upward
   to divine truth and knowledge.
Pull us upward
   to warm our hearts
     with the power to change the world.
Amen.

RESPONSIVE PRAYER (EPHESIANS 1)
For this reason we pray:
   grant us the spirit of wisdom;
enlighten our lives with hope;
   show us how to live a spiritually rich life;
bestow upon us the power to make a difference.
   We praise you, Jesus, and to you we pray.
To you is all dominion given. Amen.

BENEDICTION (ACTS 1)
We have received power from God—
   power to be witnesses in our world and nation.
We have received encouragement from the Holy Spirit—
   encouragement to witness to our communities
   in the name of Jesus until the day he returns.

BENEDICTION (LUKE 24)
Jesus lifted his hand and blessed the people.
   We have received Christ's blessing.
While Jesus was blessing them,
he was taken up into heaven.
   With hope for the future,
   we return home with great joy.

MAY 27, 2007

Pentecost Sunday

B. J. Beu

COLOR

Red

SCRIPTURE READINGS

Acts 2:1-21; Psalm 104:24-34, 35*b*; Romans 8:14-17; John
14:8-17 (25-27)

THEME IDEAS

As Jesus' disciples huddled together in fear, the Holy
Spirit entered their dwelling in rushing wind and
tongues of fire, and the Church was born. We put on
elaborate celebrations for Christmas and Easter, but
Pentecost is equally important. Without Pentecost, the
disciples would not have had the courage to go forth and
spread the gospel. The Spirit that was promised to the
prophet Joel is active in our world today, granting visions
and dreams to our old and young alike. The power of
God to create and renew life is the power of the Holy
Spirit. We see this power in the psalmist's hymn of
praise. We behold this power in Paul's discussion of
adoption in Christ through the Spirit. And we see the
promise of this power in Jesus, as he comforts his disciples before his death.

CALL TO WORSHIP (PSALM 104)

O Lord, your works are wonderful!
The earth is full of your handiwork.
When you open your hand,
we are filled with good things.
When you hide your face,
we are dismayed.
When you take away our breath,
we die and return to dust.
Put your Spirit within us, O God,
and renew us as your people.

CALL TO WORSHIP OR BENEDICTION (ACTS 2, JOHN 14)

In rushing wind, in cleansing fire,
God's Spirit has led us here.
In rushing wind, in cleansing fire,
God's Spirit has filled our hearts with longing.
In rushing wind, in cleansing fire,
God's Spirit has taken away our fear.
In rushing wind, in cleansing fire,
God's Spirit sends us out
to share Christ's love for all.

CONTEMPORARY GATHERING WORDS (ACTS 2)

Can you feel it? God is here!
In rushing wind and tongues of flame,
God's Spirit draws us here.
Can you feel it? Christ is here!
In rushing wind and tongues of flame,
Christ's Spirit washes over us.
Can you feel it? The Spirit is here!
In rushing wind and tongues of flame,
God's Spirit ignites our dreams.
God is here. Let us worship!

PRAISE SENTENCES (PSALM 104)

Sing to the Lord!
Sing praises to God with every breath we take!
Sing to the Lord!
Sing to the Lord!

PRAISE SENTENCES (PSALM 104)

Praise the Lord!
We will praise the Lord
as long as we draw breath!
Rejoice in the Lord!
We will rejoice in the Lord
as long as we draw breath!
Bless the Lord!
We will bless the Lord
as long as we draw breath!
Praise the Lord!
Praise the Lord!

OPENING PRAYER (ACTS 2)

Creator God,
on this day of Pentecost,
pour out your Holy Spirit
on each of us here today.
May the tongues of fire
that filled Christ's disciples
with courage and power,
ignite a fire in our hearts.
Set our hearts aflame,
that our young people
may have visions,
and our elderly
may dream dreams.
Blow into our lives,
and inspire us to spread the good news
of salvation in Jesus Christ, our Lord. Amen.

OPENING PRAYER (JOHN 14)
Eternal God,
  live in us
    as you live in your Son.
Draw us to yourself,
  that we may glorify you
    in all that we do.
Grant us your peace,
  and ease our troubled hearts,
  that we may have the courage
    to keep your commandments,
    proclaim your mighty works,
    and heed the teachings
      of your Holy Spirit. Amen.

BENEDICTION (ROMANS 8)
All who are led by the Spirit of God
are children of God.
As children of God,
we are also heirs.
As heirs of God,
we are heirs with Christ.
We go as God's children,
loved and blessed by Christ.

BENEDICTION (ACTS 2, ROMANS 8)
Go forth, blessed and filled with the Holy Spirit.
We go forth as God's children.
Go forth, blessed with a spirit of adoption.
We go forth as heirs with Christ.
Go forth in hope and joy.
We go forth blessed and filled with the Holy Spirit.

JUNE 3, 2007

Trinity Sunday
Bryan Schneider-Thomas

COLOR
White

SCRIPTURE READINGS
Proverbs 8:1-4, 22-31; Psalm 8; Romans 5:1-5; John 16:12-15

THEME IDEAS
Trinity Sunday is one of the few festivals that celebrate a theological concept rather than an event, and a difficult concept at that. Primarily, it is a celebration of the revelation of God. God has chosen to be made known in three persons. The historic identification of these three is Father, Son, and Holy Spirit. Contemporary efforts at making the identifications more inclusive have suggested Parent, Child, Spirit or Creator, Redeemer, Sanctifier. The demeanor of your congregation may determine which form is most appropriate.

CALL TO WORSHIP (TRINITY SUNDAY)
We come to worship God the Father, mighty creator and author of life.
Source of all life, we give you praise.
We come to worship God the Son, glorious redeemer and exalted savior.

**Grace flows from your hands
and love from your mouth.**
We come to worship God the Holy Spirit,
source of wisdom and comfort for the afflicted.
Almighty God, Three in One, we worship you!

CALL TO WORSHIP (PROVERBS 8)
O strength of Wisdom
who, circling, circled,
enclosing all
in one life-giving path,
three wings you have:
one soars to the heights,
one distills its essence upon the earth,
and the third is everywhere.
Praise to you, as is fitting,
O Wisdom.
**Wisdom of God, by your light
may we praise our maker and redeemer.**

CONTEMPORARY GATHERING WORDS (PSALM 8)
God has created the heavens above and the earth below.
**O Lord, our God, how majestic is your name
in all the earth!**
In the midst of such a wonderful creation, who are we
that God loves us and comes to be with us?
**O Lord, our God, how majestic is your name
in all the earth!**
God has placed us as caretakers of this creation
and empowers us for our task.
**O Lord, our God, how majestic is your name
in all the earth!**

OPENING PRAYER (ROMANS 5)
O God,
source of hope that does not disappoint

and love that fills our hearts,
lead us through these present days.
Give us the Holy Spirit:
to teach us endurance,
strengthen our character,
and lead us to you,
through Jesus Christ,
whose grace enables us to stand. Amen.

INVITATION AND UNISON PRAYER
(PROVERBS 8:4-7A)

Hear God's invitation to abundant life.
"To you, O people, I call,
and my cry is to all that live.
O simple ones, learn prudence;
acquire intelligence, you who lack it.
Hear, for I will speak noble things,
and from my lips will come what is right;
for my mouth will utter truth."
God of all wisdom,
source of truth,
you come to us
that we might be filled with wisdom.
Open our hearts and minds
that we might be filled
with truth and grace.
Teach us prudence of action
and intelligence of speech.
May our lives be testimonies
of your wisdom. Amen.

PRAYER OF CONFESSION (TRINITY SUNDAY,
APOSTLES' CREED)

Let us confess our historic faith.
I believe in God, the Father Almighty,
creator of heaven and earth.

Creator God, you set us as stewards over all creation,
  but we have not always been good stewards.
We have shown little regard for the creatures of creation.
We have ravaged the earth in search of natural resources
  and left the land stripped bare.
We have destroyed habitat and polluted the oceans.
In our abuse of the creation you have entrusted to us,
  we have not honored you.
  I believe in Jesus Christ, his only Son, our Lord,
    who was conceived by the Holy Spirit,
    born of the Virgin Mary,
    suffered under Pontius Pilate,
    was crucified, died, and was buried;
    he descended to the dead.
  on the third day he rose again;
    he ascended into heaven,
    is seated at the right hand of the Father,
    and will come again
      to judge the living and the dead.
God of never-ending love, you came to earth
  that we might be drawn closer to you.
You teach us to love you
  through our love for one another.
But we have not always shown this love.
Your suffering, death, and resurrection
  show us that there is nothing we can lose
  that you cannot restore.
You give us the great gift of grace.
Yet we are reluctant to share this grace with others,
  refusing to forgive sins as you commanded.
In our failure to do unto others as you have done for us,
  we have not honored you.
  I believe in the Holy Spirit,
    the holy catholic church,
    the communion of saints,
    the forgiveness of sins,

the resurrection of the body
and the life everlasting. Amen.
Sanctifying God, you refuse to give up on us,
    forever calling us back and forgiving our sins.
You provide for us a community of witness and support
    in the saints of your Church.
But we have fractured that community
    and ignored the example of your saints.
In our disregard for our brothers and sisters in Christ,
    we have not honored you.
    Forgive us, we pray,
        and teach us how to sin no more.

ASSURANCE OF PARDON

God is slow to anger and abounding with steadfast love.
In the name of the triune God, you are forgiven.

BENEDICTION (JOHN 16)

Now may the Spirit of truth guide you into all truth,
    that your life will glorify God
        and be a blessing to others.

BENEDICTION (ROMANS 5)

May the blessings of Creator God rest upon you.
May the salvation of Christ be your hope and guide.
And may the comfort of the Holy Spirit
    be with you always.

JUNE 10, 2007

Second Sunday after Pentecost
Mary Petrina Boyd

COLOR
Green

SCRIPTURE READINGS
1 Kings 17:8-24; Psalm 146; Galatians 1:11-24; Luke 7:11-17

THEME IDEAS
Today's scriptures proclaim new life in places filled with death. The gift of life occurs twice in the passage from 1 Kings—first, as meal and oil persist in a time of famine; and second, as the widow's son returns to life. The theme continues as Jesus revives the widow's son at Nain. Paul experiences a spiritual movement from death to life, as the one who once persecuted the church now proclaims the good news of life in Christ.

CALL TO WORSHIP (PSALM 146)
Praise the Lord, O my soul!
We will praise the Lord as long as we live!
God created the heavens and the earth.
God brings justice to the oppressed
and food to the hungry.
God opens the eyes of the blind
and lifts up those who are bowed down.

God cares for strangers, widows, and orphans.
Sing praise to our God.
The Lord reigns forever!
Praise the Lord!

CALL TO WORSHIP (GALATIANS 1)

God calls us on new journeys, leading us in faith.
Give us courage to answer your call, O God.
God breathes new life into places of death.
We open our hearts to receive your Spirit, O God.
God remakes our lives, calling us to service.
We welcome your transforming power, O God.
Come on the journey of faith.
We come with joy to worship the living God!

CONTEMPORARY GATHERING WORDS (1 KINGS 17, PSALM 146, LUKE 7)

Where people are in need,
God brings new life!
Where people are hungry,
God brings new life!
Where people are imprisoned,
God brings new life!
Where we see only death,
God brings new life!

CONTEMPORARY GATHERING WORDS (PSALM 146, LUKE 7)

When our hope is dead from fear and doubt,
Jesus says to us, "Rise!"
When our souls are dead to the teachings of God's word,
Jesus says to us, "Rise!"
When our eyes are dead to the needs of others,
Jesus says to us, "Rise!"
When our hearts are dead to the stirrings of joy,
Jesus says to us, "Rise!"

With God, life is stronger than death.
We worship the One who brings us new life.

PRAISE SENTENCES (LUKE 7)
Rise and sing God's praise.
Jesus gives us new life!
Jesus calls us to life.
Thanks be to God!

PRAISE SENTENCES (1 KINGS 17)
Do not be afraid. God's word is true!
God's life-giving Spirit flows through the world.
Thanks be to God!

OPENING PRAYER
Loving God,
  we gather as your people,
    hungry for your word,
    longing for your touch.
Breathe new life into our lives.
Touch us and heal our brokenness.
Make us your witnesses in the world,
  for Jesus' sake. Amen.

OPENING PRAYER
God of power and might,
  God of tenderness and truth,
  your word brings us a vision
    of a world of peace,
      where justice and righteousness prevail.
Cast out our fears and doubts
  and call us into your grace,
  that we may praise you
    all the days of our lives. Amen.

UNISON PRAYER (PSALM 146, LUKE 7)
Generous God,
  thank you for all you give us:

a world of beauty and grace,
a community of love and caring,
an opportunity for new life
    through your Son, Jesus Christ.
We pray for all who are in need:
    for victims of injustice throughout the world,
    for children who are hungry,
    for elders who are lonely and long for community,
    for men who are discouraged,
    for women who need healing.
Breathe your new life into places of despair,
    and restore all people
    to the wholeness of your love.
We offer ourselves as your people,
    ready to share your love with others. Amen.

PRAYER OF CONFESSION (1 KINGS 17)

Life-giving God,
    we are filled with fear and doubt.
We worry that we do not have enough.
We are overwhelmed by the world's problems.
We see danger everywhere.
We are blind to your work.
Give us trusting hearts.
Show us life's possibilities.
Heal the world's brokenness.
Use us as agents of change.
Remove our doubt and fear,
    and teach us to live in you. Amen.

WORDS OF ASSURANCE

God's love has power to sweep through our lives
    and wipe away our fears and doubts.
The breath of God will bring us new life.

Prayer of Confession (Galatians 1)
Compassionate God,
    we confess that we have failed you.
We have not proclaimed your word.
We have caused others to suffer.
We have been afraid to answer your call.
Forgive us, O God.
Touch us with your Spirit,
    and heal our brokenness.
Give us courage to go where you send us.
Give us wisdom to share your love. Amen.

Words of Assurance
God forgives our failures, transforms our brokenness,
    and sends us forth to serve.

Benediction (Galatians 1)
You are called by God's grace to serve the world.
Go and proclaim the good news.
In Jesus Christ we find life and hope. Alleluia!

Benediction (1 Kings 17, Psalm 146)
Go where God sends you.
    We go to serve God's people.
Work for justice for all people.
    We go to serve God's people.
Bring healing, hope, and new life.
    We go to serve God's people.

JUNE 17, 2007

Third Sunday after Pentecost
Father's Day

Rebecca Gaudino

COLOR

Green

SCRIPTURE READINGS

1 Kings 21:1-21*a*; Psalm 5:1-8; Galatians 2:15-21; Luke 7:36–8:3

THEME IDEAS

This Sunday's lessons offer us models of courage and faithfulness. Naboth stands up to corrupt royal power in order to preserve his land and all that this land means to his family. While his death is insignificant to those at the palace, God takes note and sends Elijah. In Galatians, translations usually speak of "faith *in* Jesus Christ" (vv. 16, 20), referring to our human faith. But the alternative translation, "faith *of* Jesus Christ," gets at Jesus' faith or faithfulness in giving himself for us. When we believe, our faith is interwoven with his, and he lives in us. In Luke, we meet a woman known to be a sinner who disregards religious and social etiquette to encounter Jesus. Rather than being rebuked by Jesus, she leaves with his blessing of salvation and peace.

CALL TO WORSHIP (PSALM 5)
Through the abundance of your steadfast love, O God,
we will enter your house.
Through the abundance of your steadfast love, O God,
we will bow down in awe in your holy temple.
Through the abundance of your steadfast love, O God,
we will listen to your holy word.
Through the abundance of your steadfast love, O God,
we will follow the path you lay before us.
Through the abundance of your steadfast love, O God,
we will worship you in love and gratitude.

CONTEMPORARY GATHERING WORDS (PSALM 5, 1 KINGS 21, LUKE 7)
We come from our morning papers
troubled by their stories of loss and violence.
O God, hear our sighs.
We stop in the midst of our lives—
with our own stories of regret, fear, and anxiety.
O God, hear our sighs.
We call out to you, the One who holds our lives
in powerful and loving hands:
O God, hear our sighs.

PRAISE SENTENCES (GALATIANS 2)
The Child of God loves us and gave himself for us!
We have been crucified and raised with Christ.
It is no longer we who live.
It is Christ who lives in us!
The Child of God loves us and gave himself for us!

PRAISE SENTENCES (PSALM 5)
God hears us in the morning.
God listens to the sound of our cries.
God's love for us is abundant and steadfast.
We are welcome in God's presence!

OPENING PRAYER (LUKE 7, GALATIANS 2, 1 KINGS 21)

God of our times,
    we need reminding:
when we weep over regrets,
    you accept and forgive us;
when we anguish over challenges,
    you renew us;
when we stand up to injustice,
    you encourage us,
    even in the face of death.
Remind us of your faithful, fierce, and deep love
    that accompanies us
        every moment of our lives. Amen.

OPENING PRAYER (1 KINGS 21, GALATIANS 2, LUKE 7)

You are a God of extravagance.
You love us dearly,
    even though we have trouble
        loving ourselves and others.
You call us to bold, history-changing acts,
    even though we are timid.
You move outside our social rules and norms
    and beckon us to follow,
    even though we are easily embarrassed.
Remind us anew
    of your love that frees us
        from isolation, fear, and shame.
Show us once more
    that you give us power to defeat evil,
    when we stand up with courage
        for what is right.
Be with us today,
    and do not let us forget. Amen.

UNISON PRAYER (1 KINGS 21, PSALM 5, GALATIANS 2, LUKE 7)

Your love comforts us,
  God of our lives.
In the midst of our rebellion,
  you love us still.
Your love also frightens us:
  calling us to be bold;
  calling us to walk into places of power
    and speak your truth;
  calling us to weep without shame,
    in deep love and longing;
  calling us to live anew in the life of Christ.
With your comfort, make us whole.
But do not stop challenging us,
  even when we are fearful and timid. Amen.

BENEDICTION (PSALM 5, GALATIANS 2, LUKE 7)

The abundance of God's steadfast love encompasses us.
  We go forth, embraced by God's love.
The abundance of God's steadfast love encompasses us.
  We go forth in peace.

BENEDICTION (GALATIANS 2, PSALM 5, LUKE 7)

Let us go forth in courage and strength!
  It is no longer we who live,
  but Christ who lives in us!
Let us go forth in faithfulness and love!
  Lead us, O God, in your righteousness,
  and make our way straight before us.
Go in peace!

JUNE 24, 2007

Fourth Sunday after Pentecost
Laura Jaquith Bartlett

COLOR
Green

SCRIPTURE READINGS
1 Kings 19:1-15*a*; Psalm 42; Galatians 3:23-29; Luke 8:26-39

THEME IDEAS
As the psalmist writes so eloquently, our souls long for God. Luke's story of the demons horrifies us, and yet we secretly know that we are plagued by our own demons. Like Elijah, we try to be faithful followers, but we don't always understand where to find God. These scriptures, which at first glance may seem far removed from life in the twenty-first century, do indeed speak to us here and now. When we dare to open our hearts to God's presence, we find that God has been here all along, offering us flowing streams of living water.

CALL TO WORSHIP (PSALM 42)
As a deer longs for flowing streams,
our souls long for you, O God.
 Come, drink of the living waters and be revived!
As a deer longs for flowing streams,
our souls long for you, O God.
 Come, listen for the voice of God, and be revived!

As a deer longs for flowing streams,
our souls long for you, O God.
Come, clothe yourself with Christ, and be revived!

CALL TO WORSHIP (GALATIANS 3)

Gather from the four corners of the earth,
and declare what God has done for you.
We are all one in Christ Jesus!
Gather from north and south, from east and west,
and listen for the voice of God.
We are all one in Christ Jesus!
Gather from houses and apartments, from trailers
and condos, and come drink from God's living waters.
We are all one in Christ Jesus!

CONTEMPORARY GATHERING WORDS (1 KINGS 19)

Listen to the wind! It splits mountains and breaks rocks.
Is God there?
Feel the earthquake! It shakes the foundations of the
world.
Is God there?
Watch the fire! It leaps and crackles and roars.
Is God there?
Experience the sound of sheer silence.
(Pause)
God is here!

PRAISE SENTENCES (GALATIANS 3)

In Christ Jesus, we are all children of God through faith!
There is no longer Jew or Greek, Christian or Muslim.
There is no longer slave or free, rich or poor.
There is no longer male or female, gay or straight.
For all are one in Christ Jesus!

PRAISE SENTENCES

Hope in God, our rock and our help.
The living God quenches our thirst.

The song of God is with us always.
Hope in God, our rock and our help!

SCRIPTURE LITANY (1 KINGS 19:9*b*, 11-13)

Elijah, afraid and running for his life,
confronted the Living God at Mount Horeb.
  "What are you doing here, Elijah?
  Go out and stand on the mountain
  before the Lord, for the Lord is about to pass by."
Now there was a great wind—a wind so strong
that it split mountains and broke rocks in pieces
before the Lord.
  But the Lord was not in the wind.
And after the wind, an earthquake shook the ground
to the roots of the mountain.
  But the Lord was not in the earthquake.
And after the earthquake,
a fire blazed up toward the heavens.
  But the Lord was not in the fire.
And after the fire came a sound of sheer silence.
When Elijah heard it, he wrapped his face in his mantle
and went out and stood at the entrance of the cave.
  God speaks to us in silence.
  God is still speaking.
(B. J. Beu)

OPENING PRAYER

(Follow this prayer with a time of silence.)
O God,
    our ears are open,
    and we long to hear you
        in the sheer silence.
Help us quiet the spinning of our minds,
    calm the frenetic pace of our breathing,
    and slow the pounding of our hearts.
Come to us now in the silence.
Come, Lord Jesus, come. Amen.

OPENING PRAYER

Healer God,
we come to you in our brokenness,
ready for your healing touch.
We are tormented by the demons of worry,
of stress, of too many possessions
and not enough resources.
We offer ourselves now into your care.
Heal us, nourish us,
make us one in Christ Jesus,
in whose name we pray. Amen.

PRAYER OF CONFESSION

Surprising God,
we often look for you
in all the wrong places.
We work hard on huge anthems of intricate praise,
and we forget to seek you
in the simple melody of a child.
We craft elaborate pageants full of drama,
and we forget to seek you
in the unrehearsed cry of the heart.
We work to build the best programs,
the most successful classes,
the most sought-after workshops,
and we forget to seek you
in the eyes of the lonely woman
at the bus stop.
Guide us, O God,
and open our hearts to find you
in the unexpected places of our lives.
This we pray in the name of the One who came,
not as a king, but as a baby. Amen.

WORDS OF ASSURANCE

Our hope is in God,
who offers living water to quench our souls.
Drink of this water, and never thirst again.

Hope in God,
 and be flooded with the overflowing mercy
  of God's love.

BENEDICTION

May you rest in the hope of God,
 be unified in Christ Jesus,
 and be sustained by the power of the Holy Spirit.
You belong to Christ!

BENEDICTION

Go into the world, proclaiming all that Jesus has done
for you.
 We are one in Christ Jesus!
Go into the world, ready to find God in unexpected
places.
 We are one in Christ Jesus!
Go into the world, empowered by the Holy Spirit.
 We are one in Christ Jesus!

JULY 1, 2007

Fifth Sunday after Pentecost
Robert Blezard

COLOR
Green

SCRIPTURE READINGS
2 Kings 2:1-2, 6-14; Psalm 77:1-2, 11-20; Galatians 5:1, 13-25; Luke 9:51-62

THEME IDEAS
Today's readings speak of the power of God and the power that God's people have both to live holy lives and to work to further God's reign. Second Kings references the transfer of God's prophetic power from Elijah to Elisha, and displays God's power as fiery chariots and horses of fire carry Elijah to heaven in a whirlwind. Psalm 77 is a hymn to God's saving power—a power depicted by thunder, lightning, and whirlwind. Galatians brings a new wrinkle. God's power leads to personal transformation and to the leading of holy lives by growing the fruit of the Spirit in us: love, joy, patience, and so forth. Luke's gospel illustrates restraint. Jesus rebukes the disciples for suggesting that they call down fire to consume a Samaritan village. Interestingly, Jesus takes the threat seriously and implicitly does not deny that the disciples are capable of doing this. Together, the

readings speak of the power of God that is entrusted to God's holy people—that they may live righteous lives for themselves, and that they may be workers and witnesses for God's reign.

CALL TO WORSHIP (PSALM 77)
We cry aloud to God.
God, hear our cry.
In our day of trouble, we seek the Almighty.
God, meet us here.
We will meditate on God's mighty deeds.
God, inspire our hearts and minds.
We remember God's wonders.
God, bless our world and our lives.
We pray God will deliver and redeem us.
God, deliver and save us.

CALL TO WORSHIP (GALATIANS 5)
We seek the guidance of the Spirit,
to be free in Christ and resist the yoke of slavery.
We seek the guidance of the Spirit,
to love our neighbors as ourselves.
We seek the guidance of the Spirit,
to live with self-control, gentleness, and joy.
We seek the guidance of the Spirit,
to be the people Christ calls us to be.

CONTEMPORARY GATHERING WORDS (LUKE 9)
Jesus wants us to follow him. Are you ready?
We will follow wherever Jesus goes.
God will help us on the journey.
But Jesus had no place to lay his head.
Can you let go of your security?
We will follow wherever Jesus goes.
God will help us on the journey.

But discipleship may disrupt your relationships.
Can you do that?
We will follow wherever Jesus goes.
God will help us on the journey.
But discipleship may reorder your priorities.
Are you ready?
We will follow wherever Jesus goes.
God will help us on the journey.

PRAISE SENTENCES (PSALM 77, GALATIANS 5)

What god is so great as our God?
We see God's power in thunder and wind,
in ocean tides, waterfalls, and river rapids.
We know God's power to redeem our lives,
to free us from slavery, and to make us holy.
What god is so great as our God?

OPENING PRAYER (GALATIANS 5)

Holy and loving God,
we desire for our lives
what you desire for us:
freedom, peace, joy, gentleness, self-control,
to love our neighbors as ourselves.
We pray that your Spirit
may work within us today:
guiding us, teaching us, challenging us.
Help us live by the Spirit.

OPENING PRAYER (LUKE 9)

God, we want to receive you.
Open our hearts, O God.
We want to follow you wherever you go.
Help us give up our need for control and security.
We want to proclaim the kingdom of God.
Help us put our hand to the plow and not look back.

LITANY OF CONFESSION (GALATIANS 5)

Merciful God, you called us for freedom in Christ,
but we have submitted to sin's yoke of slavery.
Have mercy upon us.
We have misused our freedom, making it an opportunity
for self-indulgence instead of loving our neighbors as
ourselves.
Have mercy upon us.
We have been jealous, angry, quarrelsome, impure,
and idolatrous.
Have mercy upon us.

WORDS OF ASSURANCE

Hear God's words of comfort.
Those who belong to Christ Jesus
have crucified the flesh
with its passions and desires.
If we live by the Spirit,
let us also be guided by the Spirit.

BENEDICTION (2 KINGS 2)

Go in peace.
May the God who gave the power of the Spirit
to Elijah, Elisha, and the disciples of old,
give this spiritual strength, courage, and vision to us,
that we may do mighty things in God's name.

BENEDICTION (LUKE 9)

May you receive God with a tender heart.
May you follow God with a steadfast vision.
May you proclaim the kingdom of God in all that you do.
May God's Spirit sustain, nourish, and guide you
on your journey.

JULY 8, 2007

Sixth Sunday after Pentecost
Erik J. Alsgaard

COLOR

Green

SCRIPTURE READINGS

2 Kings 5:1-14; Psalm 30; Galatians 6:(1-6), 7-16; Luke 10:1-11, 16-20

THEME IDEAS

On this Sunday after July Fourth, the notion that healing is a form of independence may be a rich vein to mine. Sickness and disease can force a form of captivity on people's lives. From time to time, we resist being healed because we are "used" to our life as it is. Naaman's healing at the instructions of Elisha illustrates this aspect of healing. The psalmist's rejoicing at being restored to health is a marvelous ode to joy or a thanksgiving, which is another aspect of healing. And Jesus' instructions to the seventy clearly give disciples (us) the ministry of healing. Each of today's readings requires human response and action for healing to take place. We take an active role in our own healing.

CALL TO WORSHIP (PSALM 30)

Sing praises to the Lord!
God turns our mourning into dancing!

Sing praises to the Lord!
God clothes us with joy!
Sing praises to the Lord!
God restores our health, our souls, our spirits!
Sing praises to the Lord!

CALL TO WORSHIP (2 KINGS 5, LUKE 10)

Jesus calls us to cure the sick.
Lord, help us to be healed and to be healers.
Jesus calls us to proclaim that God's kingdom is near.
Lord, help us to be instruments of thy will.
Jesus calls us to be healthy and whole.
Lord, help us turn to you, our physician, our healer.
God is in the healing business.
Thanks be to God!

CONTEMPORARY GATHERING WORDS (PSALM 30)

(These words go well immediately following the song "Lord of the Dance")
Dance, then, wherever you may be!
We come into God's presence with praise!
Dance, then, for God is here to heal us!
We come into God's presence with singing!
Dance, then, for God is faithful and true!
We come into God's presence with joy!
Dance like nobody's watching!
We come into God's presence with dance!

PRAISE SENTENCES (2 KINGS 5)

Our God is a God of healing and wholeness.
Praise God for the health we enjoy.
Praise God, whose healing is not just an outer body experience.
Praise God, who heals us from the inside out.

OPENING PRAYER (PSALM 30, GALATIANS 6)

Gracious God,
your will for all creation

is health and wholeness.
Grant to us this day
  your mercy, forgiveness, and love.
Bathe us in your Spirit,
  that our spirits, our bodies, and our souls
    may find rest and peace in you.
This we pray
  in the name of the One sent to heal us,
  Jesus Christ our Lord. Amen.

OPENING PRAYER (GALATIANS 6)

God, the source of all healing,
  touch our lives with your Holy Spirit.
Give us your peace, your mercy,
  and your forgiveness.
Mend our broken lives.
Mend our broken ways.
Help us turn away from sin,
  toward the ways that lead
    to wholeness and health.
In Jesus' name we pray. Amen.

PRAYER OF CONFESSION (2 KINGS 5)

Almighty God,
  you desire health and wholeness
    for all your creation.
Forgive us when we stay trapped
  in unhealthy ways.
Forgive us when we cling
  to our old familiar *dis-ease*.
Forgive us when we convince ourselves
  that we know better than you.
Help us trust your love and your Spirit
  to lead us on the path of new life.
In Jesus' name we pray. Amen.

BENEDICTION (LUKE 10)

Go forth as a people healed by God.
We go forth as healers into the world,
to share what God has done for us.
Go forth as a people called by God.
We go forth, called to share
what God has done for us.
Go forth to bring God's healing love to a hurting world.
May God's blessing be with us as we share what God
has done for us.

BENEDICTION (PSALM 30)

We have sung praises to God
and remembered God's goodness.
Our weeping is short, but our joy in God
lasts forever!
Go forward with the strength of God,
turning mourning into dancing.
We go into the world to bless, to heal,
and to proclaim God's love for all.

JULY 15, 2007

Seventh Sunday after Pentecost
Bill Hoppe

COLOR
Green

SCRIPTURE READINGS
Amos 7:7-17; Psalm 82; Colossians 1:1-14; Luke 10:25-37

THEME IDEAS
"Who is my neighbor?" It's such a deceptively simple question. In answer, Jesus gives us the beloved story of the good Samaritan, one of the most profound examples of how we should live out our faith in all of Scripture. By nature, we are more like the two who passed by the beaten man on the other side of the road. Indeed, our sins and indifference are clearly and vividly illustrated in the passages from Amos and Psalm 82. Paul reminds us that Christ has mercifully "rescued us from the power of darkness" (Colossians 1:13), with forgiveness and redemption, and with wisdom and understanding to know the Lord's will: to love our neighbor just as we love ourselves.

CALL TO WORSHIP (PSALM 82)
God delivers judgment in the court of heaven.
God is the true and righteous judge!
How long will there be injustice in this life?
How long will the wicked be favored?

The weak and the orphans, the destitute and the needy,
they all cry out for justice.
Rise up, Lord. Judge the earth!
All the world belongs to you!

CALL TO WORSHIP (LUKE 10)

God offers us eternal life.
**We will love the Lord our God, with all our heart,
will all our soul, with all our mind, and with all
our strength.**
God calls us to love one another.
We will love our neighbor as we love ourselves.
Let us worship the God of abundant love.
(B. J. Beu)

CONTEMPORARY GATHERING WORDS (PSALM 82, LUKE 10)

Who is my neighbor?
**The righteous and the unrighteous,
the just and the wicked.**
Who else is my neighbor?
**The rich and the poor,
the weak and the strong.**
Is anyone else my neighbor?
**The great and the small,
the arrogant and the humble.**
They are no different than I am!
You must love your neighbor as yourself!

CONTEMPORARY GATHERING WORDS (LUKE 10)

What must we do to inherit eternal life?
What is written in the Scriptures?
What do they tell us?
**You shall love the Lord your God
with all your heart, and with all your soul,
and with all your strength, and with all your mind.
And you shall love your neighbor as yourself.**

That is the right answer; it is the key to life.
But do you understand it?
We are not sure. Just who is our neighbor?
Open your eyes and see.
Your neighbor is next to you.
Your neighbors surround you!
Lord, we have been so blind.
Have mercy on us!
The Lord is gracious and merciful;
show this same mercy to all.

PRAISE SENTENCES (COLOSSIANS 1)
God has freed us from darkness!
Our lives are illuminated by God's light!
Our lives bear the fruit of our hope in Christ!
We belong to the kingdom of God!

OPENING PRAYER (COLOSSIANS 1)
Our hope is in you, Lord,
    our hearts belong to heaven.
Our hope comes from the gospel,
    the word of the truth
        that you brought to us.
May it bear abundant fruit
    in our lives.
Let the whole world
    be filled with your hope!
As we grow in faith,
    help us truly comprehend your grace, O God;
    help us understand this amazing grace,
        as we seek to lead lives worthy of you, O Lord.
In Jesus' name, we pray. Amen.

OPENING PRAYER OR PRAYER OF CONFESSION (LUKE 10)
Dear Lord,
    how often we hear of real-life good Samaritans:

those who would give the shirts off their backs,
those who would do anything and everything
to help people in need.
How ashamed we feel
when we realize how little we do
to seek justice
and to alleviate suffering
in our world.
We are amazed by our own ignorance.
We offer our hearts and hands to help, Lord.
As we feed the hungry, heal the sick,
and shelter the homeless,
may we also be fed by your bread of life,
healed by your gentle touch,
and sheltered by your indescribable love.
Amen.

PRAYER OF CONFESSION (AMOS 7)

You stand beside a wall
with a plumb line in your hand, Lord—
the wall that I have built.
What once was a straight, strong wall of protection,
a sanctuary against all that might harm me,
is now revealed as a bowed, bulging,
weak wall of separation
that I have used to conceal myself
within a dark prison of my own making.
I know that your perfect judgment
finds me wanting.
Free me, Lord;
I am my own worst enemy.
Level my feeble fortress,
and rebuild me in the strength of your love
and your forgiveness.
Lead me from my darkness
into your light. Amen.

PRAYER OF CONFESSION (LUKE 10)

We see them daily, Lord.
We see them everywhere
as we go about our business:
the weak and the helpless,
the abused and the homeless,
the victims and the vanquished.
We are no different than the men in your story—
the ones who refused to help the beaten man
on the road to Jericho.
We too have passed by those in need
on the other side of the road.
We too have refused to help
and have consciously chosen
to remain uninvolved.
Forgive our indifference.
May we become like the outcast Samaritan,
who did everything in his power
to help the suffering.
In your holy name we pray. Amen.

WORDS OF ASSURANCE (COLOSSIANS 1)

We no longer belong to the power of darkness.
We belong to the kingdom of the Son of God,
Christ Jesus, who has set us free
and forgiven our sins.
Remember the hope stored up for us in heaven—
the hope that flamed into life
when we first heard the good news;
the hope of the glory to come;
the hope we have in Christ Jesus.

BENEDICTION (COLOSSIANS 1)

Be filled with all wisdom and spiritual insight.
Lead lives pleasing to the Lord
and worthy of our calling.

Bear fruit in good works of every kind,
  as we grow in the knowledge of God.
Be strong in the glorious might of the Lord,
    who gives us power to endure everything
      with patience and joy.
Give thanks to the One
    who has rescued us from darkness,
    that we might live forever
      in the realm of light. Amen!

JULY 22, 2007

Eighth Sunday after Pentecost
Mary J. Scifres

COLOR
Green

SCRIPTURE READINGS
Amos 8:1-12; Psalm 52; Colossians 1:15-28; Luke 10:38-42

THEME IDEAS
Judgment and lamentation arise from our Hebrew Scriptures today, but the hope of Colossians brings forth the good news that, in Christ, we are all reconciled to God. Even those who have done evil deeds are brought near to God and declared "holy and blameless." What a marvelous gift! No wonder Mary simply sat at Jesus' feet and listened! And yet, it is easy to become distracted. Martha's many duties made it all too easy for her to forget the marvelous gift of Jesus' presence. In these summer months of rest, the story of Mary and Martha encourages us to remember the need for the Sabbath. The Sabbath comes as a gift, not so much as a time of rest, but rather as a time of reflection and remembrance that God is in our very midst. What a marvelous gift!

CALL TO WORSHIP (COLOSSIANS 1)
Come to Christ, the immortal One,
who is worthy of praise!

**The Creator calls us here, to proclaim the glory
of God's mysterious love!**
Come near to God, for we are welcome
through this marvelous gift of grace.
**Reconciled and made holy,
we are partners with God,
givers of love and grace.**
How great is this mystery!
How great is Christ's love!
**How great is our God!
Let us worship and praise!**

CALL TO WORSHIP (COLOSSIANS 1)

Praise the Lord, who makes us whole.
Praise our God, who calls us here!
Praise the Immortal, Invisible God!
Praise the Present, Living Christ!
Praise the Creator, who makes all things new!
Praise the Creator, who reigns above!
Praise to Christ Jesus, the fullness of God.
Praise to Christ Jesus, our Prince of Peace!
Praise to the Spirit, mysterious wind and flame.
Praise to the Spirit, flowing in our lives!
Praise our God, who calls us here!
Praise the Immortal, Invisible God!

CALL TO WORSHIP (LUKE 10)

Friend and stranger, are you distracted this day?
We come to sit at Christ's feet.
All are welcome, for God is here.
**We choose the better part—
to listen and worship in love.**

CONTEMPORARY GATHERING WORDS (PSALM 52)

Trust in the love of God that never ends!
Give thanks to the Lord, for God's love endures forever!

CONTEMPORARY GATHERING WORDS (COLOSSIANS 1)

Come near, my friends,
for Christ is here.
Christ welcomes all in love!
Come near, my friends,
for we are made whole, forgiven in grace.
God's love covers all our mistakes.
Come near, my friends,
Christ is in you, the hope of all hopes,
waiting to shine for the world!

PRAISE SENTENCES (PSALM 52)

Trust in Christ's love forever!
Thanks be to God!
Trust in Christ's love forever!
Thanks be to God!

OPENING PRAYER (AMOS 8, COLOSSIANS 1, LUKE 10)

Immortal, invisible God,
reveal yourself to us this day.
As we come into your presence
and seek your word,
show us the truth of your love.
We have wandered far and wide,
but here we sit at your feet,
listening with hope and awe.
Bring us near through your grace,
and shower us with mercy.
Feed our hunger for righteousness,
and satisfy our thirst for justice.
Nurture us with your truth,
and challenge us with your call
to spread love and peace
in the world. Amen.

CALL TO PRAYER (LUKE 10)

Whether our name is Mary or Martha,
James or John; Keesha or Maya,
Deante or Darrel, Hikare or YooCha,
JeeAhn or Kim:
Christ calls us each by name.
Leave the distractions behind,
and listen for God's voice.

OPENING PRAYER (LUKE 10)

Christ of love and friendship,
welcome us here.
Help us shed the worries of this day
and the distractions of our lives.
Center us on the truth of your love.
Open our hearts and minds
to focus on your holy word.
Strengthen us in this time of worship,
that we may leave
with the courage and the confidence
to be your people.
Help us find the energy of Martha
and the focus of Mary,
that we may be disciples
who both know and live
your law of love. Amen.

PRAYER OF CONFESSION AND HOPE (AMOS 8, PSALM 52)

God of steadfast love and faithfulness,
make us like a basket of summer fruit—
life-giving and nurturing.
Forgive us for being dried and withered.
Inject new beginnings into our lives and our faith,
even as you remember the times
we have failed.

Help us be speakers of love,
    rather than idle gossipers.
Help us be righteous and just,
    rather than selfish and evil.
And let your word flow in our lives,
    guiding all that we say and all that we do,
    that we may be your people,
    and you may be our God. Amen.

WORDS OF ASSURANCE (PSALM 52, COLOSSIANS 1)

Trust in the steadfast love of God:
    God is faithful; God is true.
Christ bring us this steadfast love,
    which is ours for the taking.
In Christ, we are forgiven!
Thanks be to God!

LITANY (AMOS 8, GALATIANS 5)

In a world where wailing abounds,
hear the righteousness of God.
    The poor are mine.
    Let us bring them hope.
In a world where we trample on the needy,
and ruin the hopes of the poor,
live the righteousness of God.
    The needy are ours.
    Let us bring them hope.
In a world where silver is valued
and poverty is scorned,
proclaim the truth of God.
    Only love endures forever.
    Let us bring God's love to all.
Love, joy, peace, faith, patience, kindness,
goodness, generosity, and self-control.

These are the fruit of God's spirit.
Let us be baskets of summer fruit!

BENEDICTION (COLOSSIANS 1)

The mystery of God is no longer hidden.
Let the mystery of love be proclaimed in our lives!
Christ is in you. You are the hope of God's glory.
Let the hope of God light our way in the world!

BENEDICTION (AMOS 8, COLOSSIANS 1)

Be fruity and fruitful followers of God!
Be lively and lovely lovers of God!
Be just who you are in justice and truth.
For we are the hope of Christ's glory!

JULY 29, 2007

Ninth Sunday after Pentecost
Mary J. Scifres

COLOR
Green

SCRIPTURE READINGS
Hosea 1:2-10; Psalm 85; Colossians 2:6-15 (16-19); Luke 11:1-13

THEME IDEAS
The contrast among today's scriptures will leave even the most accomplished worship leaders at a loss to merge these readings together. Remembering that thematic interconnection is not the point of readings during the ordinary season, the day's focus may center on the absolute devastation of losing touch with God and God's call in our lives, as depicted by Hosea. Closely related, but ending with the promise of hope and renewal, the psalmist laments this feeling of abandonment, but recalls God's steadfast love. The growth imagery in Colossians can be used to challenge one's faith community or our individual need for growth on our Christian journeys. Finally, the well-known words of Luke are packed with more questions than answers, proclaiming God's providential care in a world where hunger and hurt exist far too abundantly. Choose your scripture and enjoy the very different challenge that each offers!

CALL TO WORSHIP (COLOSSIANS 2)
Are you growing as the body of Christ?
We are rooted and built in Christ alone!
Do you believe in the power of God?
We trust in the fullness of God's grace!
Then come to the fountain of life.
We come to the nourishing waters of worship.
Come to the life-giving bread of praise.
Let us worship the One whose breath gives us life.

CALL TO WORSHIP (PSALM 85)
Surely, salvation is at hand!
God's goodness has called us here.
With reverence, we come into Christ's presence.
With joy, we sing of Christ's steadfast love.
With hope, we live as the body of Christ.
With love and faithfulness, we are melded together.
We seek justice and peace,
for these are the bonds of God's kingdom on earth.
Come, seekers of righteousness.
God's goodness has called us here!

CONTEMPORARY GATHERING WORDS (COLOSSIANS 2)
Receive the word of God.
Breathe in the truth of Christ's love!
Lift your weary limbs,
    and let the Spirit blow through your lives.
This is our spiritual worship,
    a gift of renewal and grace!

CONTEMPORARY GATHERING WORDS (COLOSSIANS 2, LUKE 11)
Are you hassled and worried?
Are you judged and condemned?

Come to Christ, who welcomes us home!
For all who seek will find.
Ask, for Christ will give freely!

CONTEMPORARY GATHERING WORDS (LUKE 11)
Are people knocking?
They're knocking at the door!
Are people knocking?
They're knocking at the door!
Open the door and let them in!
For Christ promises that when we knock,
the door shall be opened!
Open the doors of our church.
Open the doors of your hearts.
Worship welcomes all!

PRAISE SENTENCES (COLOSSIANS 2)
Christ is the root of our lives, the salvation we need!
Christ's love is all around!
Christ's love is all around!

OPENING PRAYER (LUKE 11)
Sustaining God,
   grant us our basic needs.
Where there is hunger,
   give us bread.
Where there is homelessness,
   give us shelter.
Where there is loneliness,
   give us friendship.
Forgive us for things we have done,
   and for the things we have left undone.
Where we have wronged another,
   guide us into reconciliation.
And where we have been wronged,
   guide us on the journey of forgiveness.

Save us from roads that lead to despair,
and show us the path of life. Amen.

OPENING PRAYER (LUKE 11)

Christ Jesus,
we come to your house this day,
knocking and asking
that the door be opened.
We come seeking your face,
and yearning for your presence
in our lives.
Open the doors of our hearts,
as you have opened the doors
of your church.
Lift our faces,
that we may see your face
shining upon us.
Answer our yearning,
that our restless hearts
may find rest in you. Amen.

PRAYER OF LAMENT (PSALM 85)

How long, O Lord?
How long will you hide your face?
Our world is ripped apart.
Our lives are tattered and torn.
We yearn to see your face.
We need your healing touch.
Show us your steadfast love.
Grant us your saving grace.
How long, O Lord?
How long will you hide your face?

WORDS OF ASSURANCE (PSALM 85)

Surely God's salvation is at hand!
Steadfast love and kind-heartedness will meet!

Righteousness and peace will dance in the heavens.
Faithfulness will bloom and flower.
The earth will be filled with her fragrance.
The Lord will grant goodness and grace.
God's face will shine upon us again!

BENEDICTION (COLOSSIANS 2)

Let us live our lives in Christ Jesus,
the root and foundation of our lives.
Grow up in the faith God has given us,
the faith that makes us whole.

BENEDICTION (PSALM 85)

Go forth as the faithful ones of God,
showing love and kindness to all.
Scatter seeds of righteousness and peace,
that God's kingdom may bloom anew!

AUGUST 5, 2007

Tenth Sunday after Pentecost
B. J. Beu

COLOR

Green

SCRIPTURE READINGS

Hosea 11:1-11; Psalm 107:1-9, 43; Colossians 3:1-11; Luke 12:13-21

THEME IDEAS

Today's scriptures portray God's faithfulness, even in the face of radical disobedience and unrighteous behavior. In Hosea, God laments that Israel and Ephraim, whom God suckled like a nursing mother, have turned to serve other gods. Yet God's wrath is stilled and hope is offered that the people will return from exile. The psalmist praises the Lord for God's steadfast goodness. Colossians warns us that our true lives are hidden in Christ, and we should therefore avoid reveling in earthly pleasures and unrighteous behavior. Treat everyone with equal respect, for we are one in Christ Jesus. In Luke, Jesus warns against the powers of greed, teaching us in parable to store up treasures for ourselves in heaven, not on earth.

CALL TO WORSHIP (PSALM 107)

O give thanks to the Lord,
for God is good!

God's steadfast love endures forever.
When we cry to the Lord,
God saves us from our troubles.
God's steadfast love endures forever.
When our souls faint from weariness,
God fills us with good things.
God's steadfast love endures forever.
God satisfies our hunger with good things.
God satisfies our thirst with living water.
God's steadfast love endures forever.

CALL TO WORSHIP (COLOSSIANS 3)
Let us set our minds on things that are above.
We have been raised to new life in Christ.
When Christ, who is our life, is revealed,
we will be revealed with him in glory.
We have been raised to new life in Christ.
In Christ, there is neither Jew nor Greek,
slave nor free, woman nor man.
We have been raised to new life in Christ.
Let us worship the One who is all in all,
the One who raises us to newness of life.

CONTEMPORARY GATHERING WORDS (PSALM 107)
Shout to the Lord.
Our God is an awesome God!
God's love is sure and true.
God's love never ends.
Shout to the Lord.
Our God is an awesome God!
God fills the hungry with good food,
and leads the thirsty to fountains of living water.
Shout to the Lord.
Our God is an awesome God!
God's love is sure and true.
God's love never ends.

Praise Sentences (Psalm 107)

Our God is an awesome God!
God's love endures forever and ever.
Our God is an awesome God!
God's love endures forever and ever.
Our God is an awesome God!
God's love endures forever and ever.

Praise Sentences (Colossians 3, Psalm 107)

Hidden in Christ, our lives are glorified in Jesus.
Give thanks to the Lord, for God is good!
Hidden in Christ, our lives are renewed in Jesus!
Give thanks to the Lord, for God is good!
Hidden in Christ, our lives are glorified in Jesus.
Give thanks to the Lord, for God is good!

Opening Prayer (Colossians 3)

Eternal God,
as people raised with Christ,
help us seek the things that are above,
rather than the things that are here on earth.
As you revealed Christ in glory,
our true lives remain hidden,
until revealed in your love.
Renew your Spirit within us,
and help us see your divine image
in one another.
As Christ is all in all,
help us see that all people are one
in your all-encompassing love. Amen.

Prayer of Confession (Luke 12, Colossians 3)

Loving God,
it is so easy to focus on getting our share
that we lose sight of our priorities.
Like the man who sought Jesus' help
to obtain a greater share
of his family inheritance,

we often look to you
to act as judge on our behalf.
Help us store up treasure in heaven,
rather than here on earth,
that we may be renewed in your Spirit
and revealed with Christ in glory. Amen.

ASSURANCE OF PARDON (HOSEA 11)

The God who suckled Israel and Ephraim,
leading them with cords of human kindness
and bands of love, will lead us also.
The One who forgave their waywardness
and led them out of exile,
will forgive our transgressions
and welcome us back with loving arms.

BENEDICTION (COLOSSIANS 3)

Go forth as people who have been raised
with Christ to newness of life.
Christ is our life.
Go forth as people whose lives
are hidden in the risen Lord.
Christ is our life.
Go forth as people who will be revealed in glory
when Christ's glory is revealed.
Christ is our life.

BENEDICTION (PSALM 107)

God has fed us with the words of Holy Scripture.
Fed by God's word,
our hunger is satisfied.
God has quenched our thirst with living water
from the life-giving Spirit.
Nourished by God's Spirit,
our thirst is quenched.
God has filled us with every good thing.
Renewed in Christ,
our lives are made whole.

AUGUST 12, 2007

Eleventh Sunday after Pentecost
Hans Holznagel

COLOR
Green

SCRIPTURE READINGS
Isaiah 1:1, 10-20; Psalm 50:1-8, 22-23; Hebrews 11:1-3, 8-16; Luke 12:32-40

THEME IDEAS
God's anger and God's pleasure, with individuals and with nations, are seen in today's readings. What makes God angry? Isaiah 1:10-20, the peak of argumentation in God's lawsuit against the people of the covenant, and Psalm 50, a liturgy of covenant renewal, offer strong answers. God does "not delight in," "cannot endure," is "weary of," even "hates" the people's ritual worship (Isaiah 1:10-15) and "will not accept" it (Psalm 50:9). The answer is not against worship itself (Psalm 50:8), but at what the people are doing elsewhere. What pleases God? Ceasing evil and learning to do good (Isaiah 10:16-18), and giving thanks (Psalm 50:23). Hope is also found in Luke 12, where Jesus tells the disciples it is God's "good pleasure to give you the kingdom," and urges readiness and simplicity. Finally, hope is found in Hebrews 11, where it is said that "God is not ashamed" of the faithful, courageous, forward-looking people of the covenant.

CALL TO WORSHIP (PSALM 50)

The mighty One summons us from sunrise to sunset.
Out of perfect beauty, God shines forth.
God calls to heaven and earth,
"Gather to me my faithful ones,
who made a covenant with me."
The heavens declare the righteousness of God,
the judge of people and nations.
Let us not forget God, but with thanksgiving
as our sacrifice, let us be a people of justice.
We worship the God of our salvation.

CALL TO WORSHIP (LUKE 12)

Come before God with hearts free from fear.
It is God's good pleasure to give us the kingdom.
Be ready for action and keep your lamps lit.
God comes to us like a thief in the night.
Blessed are those who are ready when the master arrives.
We are ready. Come, Lord Jesus, come.
(B. J. Beu)

CONTEMPORARY GATHERING WORDS (ISAIAH 1, PSALM 50)

Sometimes God gets angry.
People and nations don't do what they should.
Today, God reminds us of our covenant,
asking us to wash and make ourselves clean.
Learn to do good. Seek justice.
Remind us, O God, and show us the right way to go!

PRAISE SENTENCES (HEBREWS 11)

Praise God for things seen:
for stars and heavens,
for sand and seashore.
Praise God for things hoped for:
for things not seen.
Praise God for the gift of faith!

PRAISE SENTENCES (HEBREWS 11)

For mothers and fathers, strangers and foreigners,
the faithful of past generations,
we give God thanks and praise.
For their trust in God,
now entrusted to us,
we give God thanks and praise.

OPENING PRAYER (PSALM 50, LUKE 12)

Gracious God,
thank you for seeking us out,
for gathering us before you,
for not keeping silent
in the face of our need.
Thank you for calling us into account,
and for challenging us with strong words
to be a people of covenant and justice.
Thank you for assuring us
that we need not be afraid,
for it is your good pleasure
to give us your kingdom.
In courage and hope,
we come before you this hour,
to hear your Word and prepare our hearts
for the unexpected hour of your coming.
In Jesus' name we pray. Amen.

OPENING PRAYER (HEBREWS 11, LUKE 12)

Creator God,
maker of stars and seashores,
reveal your word to us this day
in which all things were made.
Redeemer God, caller of disciples,
light our lamps this day,
dress us for action,
and open the doors

of our hearts and minds.
Sustainer God,
  sender of the Holy Spirit,
  renew in us the faith of our ancestors,
  that we might claim it as our own
    in covenant with you.
In Jesus' name we pray. Amen.

PRAYER OF CONFESSION (ISAIAH 1)
O God,
  your call for justice is so clear
  that we are amazed at how easily
    we fail to hear you
      over the din of daily life.
We want to cease to do evil.
We want to learn to do good.
Yet, we rarely do all we can
  to rescue, defend, and plead
    for those in need.
As you have sought us out,
  so we seek your pardon.
Grant us courage, we pray,
  as persons, as communities, and as nations,
  to bring about the justice you desire. Amen.

WORDS OF ASSURANCE (HEBREWS 11, LUKE 12)
Faith is the assurance of things hoped for,
  the conviction of things not seen.
People of faith, God is not ashamed
  to be called your God.
By God's grace we are forgiven.
Let the church say amen.
Amen.

BENEDICTION (LUKE 12)
Have your lamps lit.
Be dressed for action.

Be generous; give alms.
Be unburdened by possessions.
Where your treasure is,
    there your heart will be also.
Go in peace. Amen.

BENEDICTION (ISAIAH 1:16-19)

Cease to do evil; learn to do good.
Seek justice; rescue the oppressed.
Defend the orphan; plead for the widow—
    and you shall eat of the good of the land.
Go in peace. Amen.

AUGUST 19, 2007

Twelfth Sunday after Pentecost
Mary J. Scifres

COLOR
Green

SCRIPTURE READINGS
Isaiah 5:1-7; Psalm 80:1-2, 8-19; Hebrews 11:29–12:2; Luke 12:49-56

THEME IDEAS
The harshness of today's passages is tempered by the hope of grace and sanctification through Christ that we find in Hebrews 12:1-2. With that hope in mind, images of carefully pruned vines and beautifully aged wine come to mind. The final scenes from the movie *A Walk in the Clouds* may inspire further images of hope in relation to today's readings.

CALL TO WORSHIP (ISAIAH 5, PSALM 80)
Let us sing a love song to God,
as God sings a love song to us.
Let us sing of amazing grace and second chances,
as Christ sings of forgiveness and mercy.
Let us sing of justice and peace,
as God calls us to live our song.
Let us sing our praises, and worship the Lord.
Let us live Christ's call, and share God's love.

CALL TO WORSHIP (HEBREWS 12)

Surrounded by saints, we are a people of faith.
Surrounded by sinners,
we are a people of forgiveness.
Saints and sinners, faithful and forgiven, we come.
Sinners and saints, called by Christ,
we come.

CONTEMPORARY GATHERING WORDS (HEBREWS 12)

This is the place where saints worship.
This is the place where sinners worship.
This is the place where faith abounds
and doubts are welcome.
This is the place where Christ perfects us
and redeems us with love and grace.
Let us join the journey and run with Christ!

PRAISE SENTENCES (ISAIAH 5, PSALM 80)

Sing of God's love!
Sing of Christ's light!
Sing of God's love!
Sing of Christ's light!

OPENING PRAYER (ISAIAH 5, PSALM 80)

God of love and justice,
plant your loving passion
for justice and righteousness
in our hearts.
Prune our selfish ambitions
to make room for compassion
and generosity.
Break down our walls of protection,
that we may welcome your light
in our lives.
Nurture us in this time of worship,

that we may answer your call
and live as your people—
a people of passion
for justice and righteousness. Amen.

OPENING PRAYER (HEBREWS 12)

We pray to you, O Christ,
for the perfection
you would instill in us.
Lead the way into our time of worship,
that we might follow
the path of the cross.
Strengthen us for the race of faith,
that we might run it
with diligence and courage. Amen.

PRAYER OF CONFESSION (ISAIAH 5, GALATIANS 5)

Christ, our Vine,
forgive us when we have not borne
the fruit of your compassion.
Dress us with your forgiveness.
Prune away our sinfulness.
Guide us into lives of justice and mercy,
that we may truly bear the fruit that is yours:
love, joy, peace, patience, kindness, generosity,
faithfulness, gentleness, and self-control. Amen.

WORDS OF ASSURANCE (HEBREWS 12)

In Christ, we are perfected.
Our sins are forgiven,
and we are made one with God!

BENEDICTION (HEBREWS 12)

Since we are supported by such a faithful God,
let us run into the world with perseverance and joy.
Let us follow Christ with passion and excitement.

Let us serve and love with kindness and mercy,
for we are the people of God!

BENEDICTION (ISAIAH 5, LUKE 12)
Do you not know?
The time is coming and now is
to build the kingdom of God.
Go into the world in pursuit of justice and peace.
Give love to the stranger
and hope to the despairing.
Go with the courage of Christ!

AUGUST 26, 2007

Thirteenth Sunday after Pentecost
Jamie Greening

COLOR
Green

SCRIPTURE READINGS
Jeremiah 1:4-10; Psalm 71:1-6; Hebrews 12:18-29; Luke 13:10-17

THEME IDEAS
Luke's gospel uses the occasion of a miracle to communicate other spiritual truths. Physical healing can lead to an understanding for the need for liberation from oppression, spiritual pain, or anything that cripples the soul. Psalm 71 similarly reverberates with a powerful prayer for deliverance. God's sovereignty, and knowledge of human beings in the womb, provides an opportunity to address such topics as sanctity of human life, individuality, calling, purpose, the family, and election. The theme of worship is strong throughout the readings: Jesus teaching in the synagogue, God as our refuge (sanctuary), God's word on Jeremiah's lips, and acceptance and freedom through a powerful God. The contrast of fear and acceptance in Hebrews and Luke reminds worshipers of the inclusive nature of the gospel, and of the attractiveness of grace.

CALL TO WORSHIP (HEBREWS 12)

We have not come to a frightening mountain
or a scary place.
We have no fear or trembling.
This is a heavenly place where angels dwell.
We have come to be the church.
We have come to the mediator between God
and humankind: Jesus Christ our Lord.
We come with reverence and awe.

CALL TO WORSHIP (HEBREWS 12)

We have come to worship our God, who comes
in blazing fire, darkness, gloom, and tempest.
We come with fear and trembling.
This is a heavenly place where angels dwell.
We have come to be the church.
We have come to worship Jesus Christ our Lord,
the mediator of a new covenant.
We come with reverence and awe.
Our God is a consuming fire.
Our God is the Lord of life and death.
(B. J. Beu)

CALL TO WORSHIP (JEREMIAH 1, HEBREWS 12)

Reach out your hand and touch our mouth, O God,
that authentic praise may flow freely from our lips.
Put your words in our mouths, O Lord,
that we might exalt you with reverence and awe.
Empower us to speak truth to the nations
and to build your kingdom here on earth.
Let it be so today. Amen. Alleluia.

CONTEMPORARY GATHERING WORDS (PSALM 71)

In a world of pain and trouble, we need a place to heal.
Here and now, we have come into the presence of God
our healer.

God is our rock and our refuge.
We seek deliverance from the evils of sickness, illness, and disease.
God is our rock and our refuge.
Let the old and the aging, the young and the innocent, the confused and the lost, turn to the Lord in hope.
God is our rock and our refuge.

PRAISE SENTENCES (HEBREWS 12)

Praise the Heavenly Father,
    the judge of the living and the dead.
Praise the Lord Jesus Christ,
    the mediator of a new covenant.
Praise the Holy Spirit,
    the fire from heaven that descends to enliven our souls.
Praise the triune God,
    whose perfect communion is worthy of our worship.

OPENING PRAYER (JEREMIAH 1, PSALM 71)

Sovereign Lord,
    you have brought your word to us today.
Before the womb's wonders were our home,
    you knew us as unique individuals,
        sacred parts of your creation.
In the mystery of the womb you protected us.
Out of the womb you have brought us.
Empower us to ministry and mission,
    with the confidence of your divine touch. Amen.

OPENING PRAYER (SEASONAL)

Lord of all creation,
    we pause before you today,
        laying our hectic lives on the altar before you.
Summer's warmth and rest are almost gone,
    and our minds are turning to the time ahead:

students and educators are thinking about school;
farmers are thinking about crops and fall harvests;
business people are thinking about profit margins
  and quarterly reports;
politicians are thinking about elections;
retailers are thinking about the holidays.
As we bow our heads before you,
  help us put aside today's worries
  and tomorrow's fears,
    that we may worship and revel
    in your presence today. Amen.

UNISON PRAYER (LUKE 13)

Lord God, we have come to hear you speak to our hearts.
Yet there is much that binds us and blunts our hearing.
As your daughters and sons, we appeal to you for
  healing and liberation—
    set us free!
From cancer, AIDS, and heart disease—
    set us free!
From diabetes, Alzheimer's, and Parkinson's—
    set us free!
From multiple sclerosis, birth defects, chemical
  dependency, and depression—
    set us free!
Through modern medicine and the miracles of science—
    set us free!
Through your healing touch, bless our lives,
  as only you can bless—
    set us free! Amen.

BENEDICTION (HEBREWS 12)

Having been warmed by the spiritual fire of our God,
  let us leave this place with unshakable courage
  and reverent awe.

BENEDICTION (LUKE 13)

On the Sabbath, Jesus was teaching in the synagogue,
and a crippled woman was healed.
Jesus set her free.
After he touched her, she rose up and praised God.
As we depart today, may God set us free.
May we lead lives worthy of our calling,
and may your praise be always upon our lips.

SEPTEMBER 2, 2007

Fourteenth Sunday after Pentecost
Rebecca Gaudino

COLOR
Green

SCRIPTURE READINGS
Jeremiah 2:4-13; Psalm 81:1, 10-16; Hebrews 13:1-8, 15-16; Luke 14:1, 7-14

THEME IDEAS
The Scripture lessons call us to choose what is worthy and life-giving. They call us to choose God and God's ways. In Jeremiah, God accuses Israel of following other gods—mere "worthless idols" (NIV) and "cracked cisterns." God alone is worthy. God alone is the "fountain of living water." Hebrews focuses on how we give life to others through acts of mutual love. Implicitly, the writer calls us to choose commitment and connection to others rather than a life ruled by greed. In Luke, Jesus bids us to choose the way of humility and radical hospitality to all, not the way of pride and the exclusion of the lowly.

CALL TO WORSHIP (PSALM 81, HEBREWS 13)
God has led us through our wildernesses.
God has led us into a plentiful land.
  God is the fountain of living water.
Come to the Water! Come to God!

We come.
"O that my people would listen to me,
O that they would walk in my ways!"
God is our strength. God is our helper.
Enter the sanctuary. Come and listen.
We come.

CALL TO WORSHIP (PSALM 81, JEREMIAH 2)
Sing aloud to God our strength!
Sing the story of our faith.
Sing of God's providential care:
water in the desert, honey from a rock.
Sing of God's sorrow at our wandering!
Sing of God's love that calls us anew.
Sing aloud to God our strength!

CONTEMPORARY GATHERING WORDS (PSALM 81, JEREMIAH 2, HEBREWS 13)
God says, "I am the fountain of living water.
I will feed you with the finest of wheat,
with honey from the rock.
You who have wandered far from me,
return to me, return to me.
You who have gathered close,
stay near, stay near.
I am the fountain of living water."
You are our strength.
You are our helper.
You are our life.
You are our joy!

PRAISE SENTENCES (PSALM 81, HEBREWS 13)
Sing aloud to God, our strength!
Shout for joy to the God of Jacob!
Offer a sacrifice of praise to God!
Let us confess God's name.

OPENING PRAYER (PSALM 81, JEREMIAH 2, HEBREWS 13, LUKE 14)

This morning, O God,
   your voice sounds into our lives again.
We are grateful to hear your call,
   for on many mornings
     we hear other voices—
       voices urging us to care only about ourselves;
       voices urging us to serve other gods:
         our work, our bank accounts, our egos,
         our peer groups, our ideologies.
By the end of the week,
   we feel trapped in our anxiety, our work, our spending,
   our need for control, and our excuses.
And then we hear your voice again,
   calling us to your healing care,
   to your spacious freedom,
   to your giving humility.
We come to rest and be fed.
Call us to your freeing love again.
Feed us now, God of our strength. Amen.

OPENING PRAYER (PSALM 81, LUKE 14)

You are the God of Mount Sinai,
   the One who proclaimed:
     "I am the Lord your God."
You are the God who summons us.
You are the God of the wilderness,
   sending bread with the morning dew
   and honey from the crags.
You are the God who loves us.
Summon us again. Love us passionately.
We pray in the name of Jesus,
   whom you summoned and loved. Amen.

PRAYER OF CONFESSION (PSALM 81, JEREMIAH 2, HEBREWS 13, LUKE 14)

Merciful God,
we find it hard to see in ourselves
the trappings our society so admires and serves—
power, wealth, and access that forget mutual love.
We fail to see our allegiance to these dangerous gods—
rushing for places of honor, scorning the humble
and lowly, supporting systems that survive on
greed and abuse.
Forgive us when we are fearful
that there is not enough.
Remind us that you are enough.
Teach us your generosity.
Teach us your world-changing humility.
Teach us your expansive love.
Transform us and heal our lives. Amen.

ASSURANCE OF PARDON

God's promises are not only to our ancestors,
they are to us as well:
"I will feed you with the finest of wheat;
with honey from the rock I will satisfy you."
In the living God, we are forgiven.

BENEDICTION (PSALM 81, HEBREWS 13)

Hear God's words of blessing.
"Listen to me! Walk in my ways!"
We hear your voice, and will follow.
"I will never leave or forsake you!"
God is our helper. We will not be afraid.

BENEDICTION (PSALM 81, HEBREWS 13, LUKE 14)

Practice humility and hospitality.
Invite the lowly to your table.
Remember the imprisoned and the tortured.

Honor your covenants.
Be content with what you have.
Love God, and walk in God's ways.
**May the way we live offer praise to God,
our helper and our strength.**
And may God feed you with the finest wheat
and the sweetest honey. Amen.

SEPTEMBER 9, 2007

Fifteenth Sunday after Pentecost
B. J. Beu

COLOR
Green

SCRIPTURE READINGS
Jeremiah 18:1-11; Psalm 139:1-6, 13-18; Philemon 1-21;
Luke 14:25-33

THEME IDEAS
The readings from Jeremiah and Psalm 139 communicate
the intimateness with which God knows our individual
and communal lives. Jeremiah warns that, just as a potter
will rework a misshapen pot, so too will God destroy
Israel to be made anew if the people do not repent. The
psalmist celebrates God's knowledge of our lives, even
before we were born. In the epistle reading, Paul exhorts
Philemon to receive back as a brother in Christ the run-
away slave Onesimus. And in the gospel reading, Jesus
warns potential followers to count the costs before com-
mitting to a life of discipleship. Forgoing one's possessions and relegating family obligations to a secondary
status are necessary for true discipleship.

CALL TO WORSHIP (PSALM 139)
O Lord, you know us completely.
You discern our thoughts from far away.

You are acquainted with all our ways.
Such knowledge is too wonderful for us.
It is so high we cannot attain it.
You formed our inward parts.
You knit us together in our mothers' wombs.
We are fearfully and wonderfully made.
Bless our time of worship,
and receive our heartfelt praise.

CALL TO WORSHIP OR BENEDICTION (JEREMIAH 18)
O Lord, you are the potter,
we are the clay.
Take our lives, O God,
and remake us anew.
Pour out your Spirit upon us,
that we may be filled with living water.
Fit us for your purposes,
that we may be wholly thine.

CONTEMPORARY GATHERING WORDS (PSALM 139)
When we try to hide, Lord,
you can always find us.
When we crawl into the darkness,
even then we do not escape your eyes.
We are tired of running, Lord.
We are here at last.
Love us as your people.
We will love you as our God.

PRAISE SENTENCES (PSALM 107)
God has made us for glory!
God's love never ends.
Christ has saved us for praise!
Christ's faithfulness never ends.
The Holy Spirit has made us whole!
The Spirit's healing never ends.

OPENING PRAYER (PSALM 139)

O Lord,
> you have searched us and known us.
You know when we seek your guidance,
> and when we flee from your presence.
Even before words are on our lips,
> you know them completely.
As we come to worship you this day,
> may our thoughts and our actions
>> be acceptable to you, O God,
>> our creator and redeemer. Amen.

PRAYER OF CONFESSION (LUKE 14)

Holy God,
> we have sought to follow you
>> without counting the costs.
Our tanks are half full.
We have hidden in the crowd,
> ignoring Christ's call
>> to pick up our cross
>> and follow him.
Help us take stock
> of our motives, our intentions,
>> and our needs for the journey,
>>> that we may finish the course in faith.
In Jesus' name, we pray. Amen.

ASSURANCE OF PARDON (PHILEMON)

In Christ, we are a new creation:
> neither slave nor free, Jew nor Greek, woman nor man.
In God's love, we are always fit for service,
> and always welcomed home.

BENEDICTION (PSALM 139, JEREMIAH 18)

The One who shaped us in the womb
loves us still.

God is the potter, we are the clay.
The One who formed our inward parts
creates us anew.
God is the potter, we are the clay.
The One who molds us in God's own image,
fashions us for glory.
God is the potter, we are the clay.
Go with God's blessings.

SEPTEMBER 16, 2007

Sixteenth Sunday after Pentecost
Mary J. Scifres

COLOR
Green

SCRIPTURE READINGS
Jeremiah 4:11-12, 22-28; Psalm 14:1-7; 1 Timothy 1:12-17;
Luke 15:1-10

THEME IDEAS
What a fascinating contrast of images between our
Hebrew and Christian scriptures today. Jeremiah proph-
esies of punishment and desolation, and the psalmist
speaks of an earth devoid of God's followers. But Paul
writes of amazing grace, and Jesus promises rejoicing in
heaven for forgiven sinners. As a sweep through salvation history, these scriptures remind us that the journey
of faith is one of failure and forgiveness—a journey
involving both judgment and mercy.

CALL TO WORSHIP (PSALM 14, 1 TIMOTHY 1)
Rejoice, O daughters of Zion!
Sing praise, O sons of Israel!
For in Christ, we are children of God.
In Christ, hope is born again!

CALL TO WORSHIP (1 TIMOTHY 1)

Immortal, invisible, God of us all ...
God of glory and grace, God of justice and love ...
we praise this great name, the great I AM of the world.
In awe we worship our marvelous God!

CALL TO WORSHIP (LUKE 15)

Come, lost sheep of the world.
Rest in the arms of God's love!
Come, folks lonely and forgotten.
Rest in the arms of God's love!

CONTEMPORARY GATHERING WORDS (LUKE 15)

Are you lost and alone?
Come to the Shepherd of Love!
Come to the Shepherd of Love!

PRAISE SENTENCES (1 TIMOTHY 1)

To God be the glory!
To God be the glory!
To God be the glory!
To God be the glory!
Now and forevermore!

OPENING PRAYER (PSALM 14)

O God of heaven and earth,
look upon us now.
Enter our hearts
and make us holy.
Grant us your grace,
and guide us in your ways.
Hear our cries.
Be with us in this time of worship,
that we may enter your grace
and live in your glory. Amen.

Opening Prayer (Luke 15)

Merciful God,
  we come like sheep to the shepherd—
    some of us following meekly,
    some of us following bravely,
    some of us wandering alone.
Gather us in.
Make us one with you,
  and make us one with each other,
  through the power of your Holy Spirit. Amen.

Prayer of Confession (Jeremiah 4, Psalm 14)

God of wind and fire,
  blow through our lives
  and release us from the baggage
    that clings to us and holds us back
      from being your people.
Lay waste the burdens that impede us.
Wash away all that weighs us down.
Free us to follow your path,
  straight and true.
Guide us into the company of the righteous,
  that we might be a refuge to the poor,
  a deliverer to the captives,
  and a friend to those who are alone.
In hope of your mercy, we pray. Amen.

Words of Assurance (1 Timothy 1)

Rejoice and be glad!
For even the greatest of sinners
  can be made whole!
Christ Jesus came to save us,
  and has given us the promise of love!

Prayer of Lament (Jeremiah 4)

A hot wind has blown through our lives.
The desert seems full of death.

We look to the heavens and see no light.
All is fruitless and dark.
In this world of sorrow and strife,
we yearn for a word of hope.
A voice whispers, "Hold fast,
the end is not yet come."
God of endings and beginnings, help us hold fast,
even in times of struggle and strife.
Guide us into new hope and new beginnings,
that we may be your people,
and you may be our God.

Benediction (Psalm 14, Luke 15)

Rejoice, my friends!
For God has restored our fortunes!
Christ has welcomed us home!
God has made us whole!

Benediction (1 Timothy 1, Luke 15)

Christ has welcomed us here.
The Spirit sends us forth.
God has called us to serve.
Christ has shown us how.
Go, servants of God.
Love and serve the Lord!

SEPTEMBER 23, 2007

Seventeenth Sunday after Pentecost
Rebecca Gaudino

COLOR
Green

SCRIPTURE READINGS
Jeremiah 8:18–9:1; Psalm 79:1-9; 1 Timothy 2:1-7; Luke 16:1-13

THEME IDEAS
Today's readings describe the sickness of our public life—sickness that evokes God's deep grief. Judah is sick-unto-death: its political, religious, and socioeconomic systems practice idolatry and render injustice (Jeremiah 5–6). Jesus tells the story of a property manager who regularly fleeces his boss. Paul writes to a young church that must learn how to present an alternative understanding of truth in the context of an empire gone awry. All the readings assert that there is but one master, one God. "Whom will you serve?" they urgently ask, for our decision makes all the difference to our individual and collective future.

CALL TO WORSHIP (PSALM 79, JEREMIAH 8)
"My joy is gone, grief is upon me, my heart is sick.
I am hurt for my poor people, I mourn, I am dismayed."
Help us, O God of our salvation. Help us!
"Is there no balm in Gilead? Is there no physician there?

Why then has the health of my poor people not been
restored?"
Help us, O God of our salvation. Help us!

CALL TO WORSHIP (PSALM 79)
We look upon our world, our neighborhoods,
our families, and see suffering and want.
How long, O Lord?
We see deep suffering, brutal violence,
destroyed homes, and ravaged nations.
How long, O Lord?
Let your compassion come quickly to meet us,
for we are brought low.
How long, O Lord?
Help us, O God of our salvation!
Help us, O Source of our hope!

CONTEMPORARY GATHERING WORDS
(PSALM 79, JEREMIAH 8, LUKE 16)
Our world is hurting in every way:
injustice in the shadows, injustice in broad daylight,
worship of wealth, worship of doctrine,
homeless people under freeways,
hungry children in our schools,
stolen pensions, destabilized nations,
politicians wined and dined, judges wooed and won,
exploding grenades, cherished grudges.
Is there any medicine to heal us? Is there any physician?
Help us, God of our salvation! Help us!

PRAISE SENTENCES (1 TIMOTHY 2)
God is our salvation.
Truly there is one God.
There is one mediator, Christ Jesus!
God is our salvation.

Praise Sentences (Psalm 79, Jeremiah 8, 1 Timothy 2)

God sees the hurt of all God's people.
Praise the God of our salvation!
God wants everyone to be saved.
Praise the God of our salvation!
God sent Jesus to give himself for all.
Praise the God of our salvation!

Opening Prayer (Jeremiah 8)

God of grief,
    you see our hurt and weep:
        "O that my head were a spring of water,
        and my eyes a fountain of tears."
Sometimes we share your grief,
    and we despair.
Sometimes we are so used to the way things are,
    that we scarcely notice.
But one day, one night, one morning,
    maybe this morning—your pain, our pain,
    our world's pain, hits us.
And we call out to you,
    "Is there a balm in Gilead? Is there healing?"
Today we wait for your answer,
    you who weep for us and with us. Amen.

Opening Prayer (Psalm 79, Jeremiah 8)

God of our salvation,
    you see your world laid waste
        with false worship, injustice, and indifference,
        and we tremble at your anger.
Only in your tears,
    born out of vast love,
    do we find hope.
Open to us the way of your tears—
    the way that leads us back to your love.

Teach us to serve you and you alone,
that you may deliver, forgive,
and renew our world at last. Amen.

PRAYER OF CONFESSION (PSALM 79, JEREMIAH 8, 1 TIMOTHY 2, LUKE 16)

We confess that we find your medicine hard to swallow.
The quick fixes of this world are so much more pleasant,
leaving us free to go back to our usual routines.
But your medicine is powerful.
And if we take it, it will remake and renew our lives.
It will reorient us to you and to you alone.
Turn us toward your love for justice and true worship.
Forgive our sins, for which you weep.
Forgive our hesitation.
Grant us courage to choose you as our physician,
and to serve you and you alone. Amen.

ASSURANCE OF PARDON

The God of our salvation,
the God who weeps for us and for our world,
desires everyone to be saved.
Christ Jesus, a human like us,
gave himself as a ransom for all.
Through the love of the one God
and the one mediator,
we are forgiven.

ASSURANCE OF PARDON

The God of our salvation,
the God who weeps for us and for our world,
is the God whose compassion
comes speedily to meet us,
and to forgive us. Amen.

BENEDICTION (1 TIMOTHY 1–2, LUKE 16)
Be faithful with little.
Be faithful with much.
Be faithful with what belongs to another.
Be faithful with what is your own.
Serve only one master.
There is one God.
We will serve this God alone.
And may the grace, mercy, and peace of the one God
be with you. Amen.

BENEDICTION (JEREMIAH 8, 1 TIMOTHY 2, LUKE 16)
Is there a physician who can heal us and our world?
The one true God can heal us.
Is there a balm in Gilead?
The one true God can heal us.
Look to God for your healing and renewal,
and for the healing and renewal of our world. Amen.

SEPTEMBER 30, 2007

Eighteenth Sunday after Pentecost
B. J. Beu

COLOR
Green

SCRIPTURE READINGS
Jeremiah 32:1-3*a*, 6-15; Psalm 91:1-6, 14-16; 1 Timothy 6:6-19; Luke 16:19-31

THEME IDEAS
In today's readings from Psalm 91 and Jeremiah, we see the fulfillment of God's promises: return from exile, hope of new beginnings, and the promise of new life springing from the ground. The New Testament readings focus on the trappings of wealth and the temptation to put our trust in money rather than in God. Those who are wealthy have a responsibility to share their riches with the poor. Wealth is an opportunity for works of generosity. Paul and Jesus warn that hoarding our riches has eternal consequences.

CALL TO WORSHIP (PSALM 91)
God is our refuge and our fortress.
In God, we place our trust.
When we are weary,
God lifts us up on wings like eagles.
When we are faced with deadly peril,

God rescues us from the snare of the fowler.
Come before the Lord with joy and longing.
God is our hope and our salvation.

CONTEMPORARY GATHERING WORDS (PSALM 91)
God protects us from harm.
We rejoice in the shelter
of the Most High.
God lifts us up when we fall.
We rejoice in the shadow
of the Almighty.
God delivers us from evil.
We rejoice in the presence
of the Lord.
Come, let us worship the Holy One.
We worship the living God,
our hope and our salvation!

PRAISE SENTENCES (PSALM 91)
We live in the shelter of the Most High!
Praise be to God!
We rest in the shadow of the Almighty!
Praise be to God!
We soar upon the wings of God's love!
Praise be to God!
We rest in the safety of Jesus' arms!
Praise be to God!

OPENING PRAYER (1 TIMOTHY 6, LUKE 16)
O God,
    you are righteous and just,
    and call us to share our riches
        with the poor.
Like the rich man
    who feasted sumptuously every day,
    while Lazarus lay hungry

and dying outside his gate,
we are easily trapped by desires
that lead to our ruin and destruction.
Help us be rich in good works,
rather than in earthly treasures.
Teach us to be generous
and ready to share all we have
with those in need.
Help us take hold of the life
that really is life. Amen.

PRAYER OF CONFESSION (1 TIMOTHY 6)
Creator God,
in our eagerness for wealth and riches,
we have wandered away from you
and pierced ourselves with many pains.
Help us be content with what we have,
for we brought nothing into this world
and can take nothing from it when we die.
Keep our focus on the ways of life:
righteousness, godliness, faith, love,
endurance, and gentleness.
Help us fight the good fight in faith,
that we might take hold of eternal life
and taste the sweet nectar of your salvation.
Amen.

ASSURANCE OF PARDON (PSALM 91)
Hear God's words of hope:
"Those who love me, I will deliver....
When they call to me, I will answer them....
With long life I will satisfy them,
and show them my salvation."

BENEDICTION (1 TIMOTHY 6)
God sends us forth with the promise of eternal life.
We will fight the good fight and live our faith.

God sends us forth with the promise of heavenly riches.
We will fight the good fight and live our faith.
God sends us forth to be rich in good works.
We will fight the good fight and live our faith.
Go with God's blessings.

BENEDICTION (PSALM 91, 1 TIMOTHY 6)

In the shelter of the Most High,
we dwell secure.
In the shadow of the Almighty,
we rest in safety.
Upon the wings of God's love,
we fly safely above the storm.
In the unapproachable light of the living God,
we no longer fear the shadow of death.
With the blessings of the One
who is our hope and our salvation,
we go forth to take hold of the life
that really is life.

OCTOBER 7, 2007

Nineteenth Sunday after Pentecost
World Communion Sunday

Bryan Schneider-Thomas

COLOR

Green

SCRIPTURE READINGS

Lamentations 1:1-6; Psalm 137; 2 Timothy 1:1-14; Luke 17:5-10

THEME IDEAS

It is important to note that World Communion Sunday is not a special Sunday observed by all denominations. For many churches, communion is celebrated every Sunday. As a result, the lectionary texts for this day do not necessarily support the theme. The purpose of World Communion Sunday is to emphasize the unity of the Church. Thus it is an appropriate Sunday to host an ecumenical event or invite an ecumenical representative or preacher. The worship suggestions for this Sunday are divided between two themes: lament and World Communion Sunday.

CALL TO WORSHIP (WORLD COMMUNION SUNDAY)

With Christians around the world,
we gather together.

To worship the God in which we are one,
we gather together.
To share in the one bread and body, to partake in the one
cup of the new covenant,
we gather together.

CALL TO WORSHIP (LUKE 17)

In a broken world,
Lord, increase our faith.
In broken lives,
Lord, increase our faith.
In broken relationships,
Lord, increase our faith.
We cry "increase our faith,"
but you have already given us the power
to heal our wounds.
Open our eyes today
to the faith that lies within.

CALL TO WORSHIP (LAMENTATIONS 1, LUKE 17)

The disciples cried, "Increase our faith!"
We can do all things in Christ who strengthens us.
The road ahead seems hard, and we feel inadequate
for the journey.
Yet, in all things, we are more than conquerors,
through Christ who loves us.
We are afraid, weak, and uncertain.
God does not give us a spirit of fear,
but rather a spirit of power and love.

CONTEMPORARY GATHERING WORDS (WORLD COMMUNION SUNDAY)

In Jesus, all Christians are one body.
But we feel isolated from one another,
separated by customs and beliefs.
In Jesus, all Christians are one body.

But we do not worship alike,
and we speak different languages.
In Jesus, all Christians are one body.
Come share the Lord!
(B. J. Beu)

PRAISE SENTENCES (WORLD COMMUNION SUNDAY)

Praise God who gives us the bread of life.
Praise Christ who unites in the breaking of the bread.
Praise the Spirit who makes us one.
(B. J. Beu)

OPENING PRAYER (LAMENTATIONS 1, PSALM 137)

Gentle Savior,
    we often feel afflicted
        by the woes of this world.
We find it difficult to praise you
    in what feels like a foreign land.
As a mother nurses her child's pain,
    you care for us,
        filling us with grace, mercy, and peace.
Turn not your ear from us,
    but hearken to our call and our tears.
Fill us with joy, restore our hearts,
    and raise our voices
        with your praise once more. Amen.

OPENING PRAYER (WORLD COMMUNION SUNDAY)

Lord Jesus Christ, you set a table for us in the wilderness,
    inviting us to share a feast of celebration.
        As we come together,
            may we be reminded that we feast
                not only with those present in this place,
                but with Christians in all times and places.

**Open our hearts to one another,
that we may truly be one. Amen.**

A Lament (Lamentations 1, Psalm 137, 2 Timothy 1)

Although Jesus is named the Prince of Peace,
we see countries and individuals destroyed by war.
Violence destroys lives in our streets and schools.
How can we sing God's song in a land of violence?
We are told to feed the hungry and clothe the poor,
but day by day, more die of starvation, and poverty
still plagues us.
How can we sing God's song in a land of affliction?
Jesus crossed the land healing the sick. Modern medicine
heals many, but diseases continue to threaten us,
leaving us looking for answers.
How can we sing God's song in a land of illness?
The apostle Paul called the Church the body of Christ,
in which there was union, not division, but the Church
fights with itself, excluding some and condemning others.
How can we sing God's song in a broken land?
We wait, O Lord, how long must we wait?
We feel empty, afraid, distressed, weak, and vulnerable.
Our eyes grow cloudy with tears.
**But our eyes are set upon you. Only in you
may our hope be renewed like the rising sun.**
God recalls your tears and will fill you with joy.
Rekindle God's gift within you, for God did not give you
a spirit of fear, but rather a spirit of power and love.

Benediction (Lamentations 1)

Though fear is not gone,
there is hope.
Though violence persists,
there is love.
Though death threatens,

there is promise.
Though all is not right,
God hears our cry and blesses us
with grace through Christ.

BENEDICTION (WORLD COMMUNION SUNDAY)
Together we have worshiped as one body
and shared the feast of Christ.
We have been knit together in Christ's love.
Together we serve Christ in this world.
With sisters and brothers around the world,
we work together.

OCTOBER 14, 2007

Twentieth Sunday after Pentecost
Laura Jaquith Bartlett

COLOR
Green

SCRIPTURE READINGS
Jeremiah 29:1, 4-7; Psalm 66:1-12; 2 Timothy 2:8-15; Luke 17:11-19

THEME IDEAS
As I write this, I hear my younger daughter singing tunelessly at the top of her lungs. Her song selection is varied, to say the least: "Go, Tell It on the Mountain," "Kum Ba Yah," "Come, Come, Everybody Worship," and "John Jacob Jingleheimer Schmidt." She weaves snippets of each seamlessly into a never-ending song of praise. That is exactly what these scriptures do. Each one presents a snapshot of faith; together they form a collage of the grace of God. Exile and salvation, gratitude and endurance—all these are part of the fabric of our faith, and we are invited to bring all our experiences together as we make a joyful noise to God.

CALL TO WORSHIP
Amidst the hustle and bustle of daily life,
we come together to worship.
Make a joyful noise to God, all the earth!

Juggling schedules, balancing day planners,
we commit to this sacred time of praise.
Make a joyful noise to God, all the earth!
Longing for the companionship of others,
drawn by God's promise of love, we come.
Make a joyful noise to God, all the earth!
Young and old, weary and energetic,
we come together to worship the One
who brings us here.
Make a joyful noise to God, all the earth!

CALL TO WORSHIP (2 TIMOTHY 2)

If we have died with Christ,
we will also live with Christ.
If we endure with Christ,
we will also reign with Christ.
If we deny Christ,
Christ will also deny us.
If we are faithless,
Christ remains faithful. Alleluia!

CONTEMPORARY GATHERING WORDS (PSALM 66, *THE MESSAGE*)

All together now—let us give God a hand!
(Congregation applauds)
Sing songs to the tune of God's glory.
Set glory to the rhythms of God's praise.
Give God a thunderous welcome!
God has set us on the road to life.
All together now—let us give God a hand!
(Congregation applauds)

PRAISE SENTENCES (PSALM 66)

God's deeds are awesome!
All the earth worships the name of God.
God has tested us, and given us burdens,
yet God has brought us to this oasis of Love.

OPENING PRAYER

Dear God,
  we gather to sing praises to your name.
Through good times and bad,
  through darkness and haze,
  you remain with us.
Your faith in us never wavers,
  and we pray this day
    that you might strengthen our faith.
Give us hearts filled with thanksgiving
  for your many blessings.
Tune our very lives,
  that we might sing our love for you
    each moment of the day.
In Christ's name we pray. Amen.

OPENING PRAYER

Awesome God,
  we come to you with thanksgiving and joy.
We come to praise your name,
  not because "it's the thing to do,"
  but because we simply cannot keep quiet.
In spite of our faltering faith,
  you continue to stick with us.
Your love never abandons us,
  even in the darkest of times.
You fill our lives
  with the wonders of your boundless mercy.
How can we keep from singing your praise
  and shouting with joy?
Alleluia, amen!

PRAYER OF CONFESSION

Gracious God,
  you have filled our lives with blessings,
  but our gratitude too often falls short.
We are quick to complain about our many burdens,

but slow to remember our riches.
We are so overwhelmed by the stresses in our lives,
    that even saying "thank you" seems too great an effort.
Energize us with your good news, O God.
Set our feet to dancing with the rhythms of your grace,
    that we may rediscover our faith.
Sing to us with the melody of your love,
    that we might throw off the burden of weariness,
    and join with you in the music of praise. Amen.
(As unspoken prayers continue, musicians may play a familiar hymn of assurance, such as "Amazing Grace" or "Freely, Freely.")

WORDS OF ASSURANCE (2 TIMOTHY 2)

When we are faithless, God remains faithful.
Nothing we do can shake God's faith in us.
Make a joyful noise to God, all the earth!

BENEDICTION

May the awesome God of all creation
    give you the melody of praise.
May the Christ of our salvation
    give you the rhythm of wholeness.
And may the Spirit of holiness
    give you the harmony of faith.
Go from this place
    to sing and dance the good news
        throughout your life!

BENEDICTION

Go out in the world, energized by God's joy.
    We go to be joyful!
Go out in the world, spreading the message
of God's great deeds.
    We go to be noisy!
Go out in the world, thankful for the ever-present love
of God.
    We go to proclaim our faith throughout the earth!

OCTOBER 21, 2007

Twenty-first Sunday after Pentecost
B. J. Beu

COLOR
Green

SCRIPTURE READINGS
Jeremiah 31:27-34; Psalm 119:97-104; 2 Timothy 3:14–4:5;
Luke 18:1-8

THEME IDEAS
The inspiration of Scripture, the value of holding fast to
God's teachings, the need to keep the faith, and God's
promise to put a new covenant in our hearts—tie these
scriptures together. Jeremiah, the psalmist, and Paul all
attest to the value of following and meditating upon
God's teachings. Luke adds the admonition from Jesus to
constantly bring our petitions before God, who will hear
and hearken to our pleas for justice.

CALL TO WORSHIP (PSALM 119)
O God, how we love your teachings!
We meditate on them day and night.
Your commandments make us wiser than our enemies.
Your precepts keep our feet from evil ways.
How sweet are your words in our mouths.
They are sweeter than honey.
Let us worship the One who guides our lives.
We worship the One who leads us into life.

CALL TO WORSHIP OR BENEDICTION (JEREMIAH 31)

Hear the good news:
we are a people of a new covenant.
Proclaim the good news:
God will write the ways of life in our hearts.
Be the good news:
we are God's people,
and the Lord is our God.

CONTEMPORARY GATHERING WORDS (PSALM 119, 2 TIMOTHY 3)

God, your teachings are awesome.
How we love to study your word!
When we are lost,
your teachings guide and save us.
When others seek to lead us astray,
your word leads us into truth.
Like the sweet taste of honey
are your words to our lips.
Sweeter than candy
are your teachings in our mouth.
Your sacred word saves us
through faith in Christ Jesus.
Thank you, Lord.
Your teachings are awesome!

PRAISE SENTENCES (JEREMIAH 31)

God is in our hearts!
God is in our lives!
God is in our world!
Thanks be to God!

PRAISE SENTENCES (LUKE 18)

God is faithful!
Worship the One who hears our pleas.

God is faithful!
Worship the One who brings justice to our world.
God is faithful!
Worship the One who inspires our faith.

OPENING PRAYER (JEREMIAH 31)

Everlasting God,
   you chart the course of our lives.
You watch over us:
   to pluck up and break down
      our errant ways,
   to build up and plant new possibilities
      for life in your Spirit.
Fulfill your promise
   to make a new covenant with us.
Put your teachings
   in our very hearts.
Be our God,
   that we may be your people—
      a people who know you
         and who keep your ways. Amen.

OPENING PRAYER (2 TIMOTHY 3)

God, our rock and our foundation,
   in the sacred writings
      we have known since our childhood,
   you have put before us
      the ways of life and death.
Keep our hearts tuned
   to the inspiration in your word,
   that we may use Scripture wisely:
      for teaching, for reproof, for correction,
      and for training in righteousness.
Keep our minds focused on sound doctrine,
   and keep our ears from itching
      for teachings that suit our selfish desires.

May we stay rooted in your truth,
through Jesus Christ our Lord. Amen.

BENEDICTION (2 TIMOTHY 3:14-15, 4:2)

Continue in what you have learned and firmly believed,
knowing from whom you learned it,
and how from childhood you have known
the sacred writings that are able to instruct you
for salvation through faith in Christ Jesus.
Proclaim the message you have heard.
Hold fast to your faith,
and be the people of God.

BENEDICTION (PSALM 119)

Taste and see that the Lord is good.
God's blessings are sweeter than honey.
Keep your feet from wandering down the wrong paths.
God's precepts give us understanding.
We will forsake every false way.
Taste and see that the Lord is good.
God's blessings are sweeter than honey.

OCTOBER 28, 2007

Twenty-second Sunday after Pentecost
Reformation Sunday
Rebecca Gaudino

COLOR
Red or Green

SCRIPTURE READINGS
Joel 2:23-32; Psalm 65; 2 Timothy 4:6-8, 16-18; Luke 18:9-14

THEME IDEAS
Today's scriptures are about a God who enters our struggles and who brings rejoicing. The post-exilic Jewish community, called earlier by Joel to fasting and weeping (2:12), hears the glad news that God will rescue them and lavish them with plenty. Paul's many trials fade in significance before the recognition of God's presence and plans that reach even beyond his death. A despised tax collector leaves his open-air confessional feeling lighter; his sins are forgiven. Our willingness to admit our defeat and failure, and our willingness to call upon God to enter our struggles, are met with God's abundant love and provision.

CALL TO WORSHIP (PSALM 65, LUKE 18)
Almighty God, you are the hope of all the earth
and the farthest seas!

You silence the roaring of the seas,
and the tumult of the peoples.
You are the hope of all the earth and the farthest seas!
When our sin overwhelms us, you forgive us.
You are the hope of all the earth and the farthest seas!
**You visit the earth and water it, softening it
with showers, blessing its growth.**
You are the hope of all the earth and the farthest seas!
**Happy are those you invite to live in your courts,
reaping the goodness of your house and your temple.**

CALL TO WORSHIP (JOEL 2)

Children of Zion, God has dealt wondrously with us.
Where we have known drought,
**God has poured down abundant rain
and filled our barns with grain,
our vats with wine and oil.**
When we have thought there was no sign of God,
**God has poured out the Holy Spirit on all flesh,
even on our sons and daughters, our young and old.**
Children of Zion, God has dealt wondrously with us.
We rejoice in our Sovereign God!

PRAISE SENTENCES (PSALM 65, 2 TIMOTHY 4)

Be glad and rejoice in your God.
To God be the glory, forever and ever!
God silences the tumult of our world.
To God be the glory, forever and ever!
God stands by us and gives us strength.
To God be the glory, forever and ever!

PRAISE SENTENCES (PSALM 65)

Happy are those you choose and bring near
to live in your courts.
Hear our praise, O God!
You answer our pleas with awesome deeds

and deliverance.
Hear our praise, O God!
You are the hope of all the earth and all the seas.
Hear our praise, O God!

OPENING PRAYER (PSALM 65, 2 TIMOTHY 4, LUKE 18)
Gracious God,
all week we have been fighting the good fight,
running the race, and keeping the faith.
And today we need your care,
for we must go out
and strive again next week.
Silence the tumult in our lives.
Lift from us all sin and defeat.
Pour your Spirit upon us.
Water the furrows of our lives
with your softening showers.
We wait in the goodness of your house,
for your merciful and generous care. Amen.

OPENING PRAYER (JOEL 2, PSALM 65)
We are overwhelmed with your generosity, O God.
Morning is here once again.
We have risen from sleep once again.
The earth turns reliably.
The seasons come and go.
The rains swell and depart.
Our crops grow and are harvested.
We eat and know plenty.
Creator, we give you thanks.
Even so, we ask another gift of you this morning.
O God who answers our prayers:
satisfy us with the goodness of your presence
in this place. Amen.

UNISON PRAYER (REFORMATION SUNDAY)

(Feel free to incorporate names significant to your congregation. As a variation, use several voices rather than the simple leader-congregation response format.)
God of our history, God of the Church,
God of *this* church,
  we thank you for your generous Spirit,
  poured out on all the faithful
  who have served you to this day.
For those who have endured,
even in the lion's mouth;
  for those who have believed
  in your ever-renewing spirit;
for those who have refused glory
for your Child's humility;
  for those who have opened
  long-closed windows for fresh air;
for those who have been steadfast
in the struggle for your kingdom,
  we give you thanks and praise.
Today, we all remember and celebrate
the founders of our Reformation faith—
Martin Luther, John Wesley, John Calvin.
But we also remember and celebrate
those from our ranks who keep our faith alive—
  (include names of congregation's reformers).
God of history, pour out your Spirit still,
  on us, on young and old, on all,
  for you alone are the hope of all the earth.
May your kingdom come. Amen.

BENEDICTION (PSALM 65, JOEL 2, 2 TIMOTHY 4)

Go forth knowing that God is in our midst,
Deliverer, Answerer of Prayers, Steadfast Companion,
Savior!
  To God be the glory, forever and ever!

BENEDICTION (2 TIMOTHY 4)

Fight the good fight; finish the race; keep the faith!
To God be the glory, forever and ever.
God will rescue you from the lion's mouth.
God will stand by you and give you strength and honor.
To God be the glory, forever and ever.

NOVEMBER 1, 2007

All Saints Day
Robert Blezard

COLOR

White

SCRIPTURE READINGS

Daniel 7:1-3, 15-18; Psalm 149; Ephesians 1:11-23; Luke 6:20-31

THEME IDEAS

Today's readings define saints not only as God's faithful, but also as the dispossessed and powerless among the people of the earth. Daniel proclaims that while mighty beasts may rise from the earth, it is God's holy ones who will possess the kingdom forever. Who are these people? Psalm 149 says that God will adorn the humble with victory and arm them with swords to smite the mighty. Ephesians talks about the rich inheritance promised to God's faithful saints. Finally, the beatitudes in Luke's gospel make God's message clear: the saints are the poor, the hungry, the weeping, and the hated. These are the blessed ones of God.

CALL TO WORSHIP (EPHESIANS 1)

Come, come know the Lord our God.
God desires to enlighten the eyes of our heart.

God longs to give us hope, and show us the rich
inheritance of the saints.
Amen.

CALL TO WORSHIP (PSALM 149)

Let us worship the Almighty!
Our voices rise with words of praise!
Let us worship the Almighty!
Our feet dance with expressions of thankfulness!
Let us worship the Almighty!
Our music and song rejoice in God's name!

CONTEMPORARY GATHERING WORDS (LUKE 6)

Come! Christ welcomes the poor.
God gives us the Kingdom.
Come! Christ welcomes the hungry.
God fills us with good things.
Come! Christ welcomes those who weep.
God makes us smile and laugh.
Come! Let us worship Christ.
God's blessings flow freely to us.

PRAISE SENTENCES (PSALM 149)

Pour out your hearts, and sing to God a new song.
Praise God in this house of prayer!
Play your music, move your feet in dancing.
Praise God in this house of prayer!
For God has done wonderful things for us.
Praise God in this house of prayer!

OPENING PRAYER (LUKE 6)

Gracious God,
  you pour out your blessings
    on the poor and downtrodden;
  you arm the powerless
    with the sword of justice;

you inspire your saints
    to right the wrongs in our world.
As we gather in this place for worship,
    grant us poverty and humility,
    that we may receive your blessings
        and the power to accomplish your will
        for our lives and the world. Amen.

OPENING PRAYER (EPHESIANS 1)

God of light,
    you have promised wisdom and revelation
        to those who put their faith in you.
Help us have that faith, O God.
Enlighten our hearts,
    that we may know the hope and the riches
        of your inheritance among the saints. Amen.

PRAYER OF CONFESSION (LUKE 6)

Woe to us, O God.
We are a people who are rich now.
Woe to us, O God.
We are a people who are full now.
Woe to us, O God.
We are a people who laugh now.
Show us your mercy, O God, and deliver us.
Teach us. Transform us. Forgive us.

WORDS OF ASSURANCE OR BENEDICTION (EPHESIANS 1)

You have heard the word of truth,
    the gospel of your salvation.
Those who believe and choose life will live.
You have been marked with the seal of the Holy Spirit.
Trust in God's promises and go in peace.

BENEDICTION (LUKE 6)

May the God of all creation,
    who blesses the poor, the hungry,

the sorrowful, and the hated,
pour blessings upon you,
and grant you the inheritance of the saints.

BENEDICTION
Go forth in strength,
knowing the hope to which God has called you,
knowing the glorious inheritance
God has reserved for the saints,
and the power God has bestowed
for those who believe,
through Christ our Lord.

NOVEMBER 4, 2007

Twenty-third Sunday after Pentecost

Mary J. Scifres

COLOR
Green

SCRIPTURE READINGS
Habakkuk 1:1-4; 2:1-4; Psalm 119:137-144; 2 Thessalonians 1:1-4, 11-12; Luke 19:1-10

THEME IDEAS
Watching and waiting begins to surface as our ordinary season nears its intersection with the season of Advent. As November begins rushing toward December, focusing worship on watchfulness and preparation can help our congregations receive the onslaught of early Christmas tidings that come from television, stores, and friends. Let these scriptures be a reminder that those who watch and wait patiently are rewarded with life-changing visions and encounters with Christ in our midst.

CALL TO WORSHIP (HABAKKUK 1–2)
Stand at your watchpost.
Wait for the Lord.
We wait and we watch.
Christ is surely coming!
Speak of your hope.
Proclaim your faith.

The time is coming and now is.
Christ is coming soon!
Christ comes. Christ calls.
Come, let us worship the Lord.

CALL TO WORSHIP (2 THESSALONIANS 1)
With steadfast love and growing faith,
we come as the body of Christ.
With prayers of hope and songs of joy,
we come to worship God.
Give thanks, my friends, for the call we have been given.
Praise and glory to the One who has called us!

CONTEMPORARY GATHERING WORDS (LUKE 19)
Christ calls to one, Christ calls to all.
I am coming to your house today!
Christ calls to you, Christ calls to me.
I am coming to your house today!
Christ has called. We have heard.
Let us worship with joy and praise!

PRAISE SENTENCES (PSALM 119)
Our God is an awesome God,
righteous and just, loving and true.
Our God is an awesome God!

OPENING PRAYER (PSALM 119, LUKE 19)
Gracious God,
   we come seeking to know you more.
We yearn to see your face
   and to walk at your side.
Look into our hearts,
   and see our deepest needs.
Lift us into new life,
   that we may follow in your ways,
   and walk with you
      all the days of our lives. Amen.

OPENING PRAYER (HABAKKUK 1–2)
We watch. We wait. We seek a vision.
Hear our prayers, O God.
Sense our deep yearning for you,
    even in the silence of our hearts.
Speak your word.
Proclaim your truth.
Open our eyes and our ears,
    that we may see and hear you now.
Amen.

PRAYER OF CONFESSION (LUKE 19)
Christ of new beginnings,
    we know that you welcomed sinners
        and ate with outcasts.
Does that mean you will welcome us as well?
When we wander away,
    will you welcome our hesitant return?
When we forsake commitments,
    and neglect your call to justice,
        will we be forgiven as readily as Zacchaeus?
God of endless love,
    welcome us into your arms of forgiveness.
Shower us with mercy when we need it most.
Help us respond as faithfully,
    as trustingly, and as generously,
    as a small tax collector
        who climbed out of a tree
            to become your disciple. Amen.

WORDS OF ASSURANCE (LUKE 19)
Today, salvation has come to this house,
    because we are the children of God.
Christ came to seek out and to save the lost.
There is nothing lost that cannot be found.
My friends, we are found.
In the name of Jesus Christ, we are forgiven!

PRAYER OF COMMITMENT (LUKE 19)

Generous God,
  receive the gifts we now return to you.
Receive the commitments we make,
  as we lay our lives before you.
Let our gifts and our lives
  be a means of grace in the world.
May the poor be cared for, the hungry fed,
  and the homeless housed.
May your word be nurtured and scattered
  throughout our neighborhoods, our communities,
  and our world.
And may your salvation come,
  not only into our lives,
  but into the lives of all
    who walk on this earth.
In Christ's name, we pray. Amen.

BENEDICTION (HABAKKUK 1–2)

Keep watch, my friends!
Christ is coming soon!
  We will keep watch and wait!
  God will not tarry.
Live by your faith,
for Christ is with us.
  We will watch and love!
  The kingdom is here!

BENEDICTION (2 THESSALONIANS 1)

Go with thanksgiving for all God has done.
  We go with hope for all Christ will do.
Go with joy for the Spirit is with us.
  We go into the world with steadfast love.

NOVEMBER 11, 2007

Twenty-fourth Sunday after Pentecost
B. J. Beu

COLOR
Green

SCRIPTURE READINGS
Haggai 1:15b–2:9; Psalm 145:1-5, 17-21; 2 Thessalonians 2:1-5, 13-17; Luke 20:27-38

THEME IDEAS
Today's scriptures proclaim hope for the future. Haggai comforts those who remembered Solomon's temple in its glory days, saying that the new temple will be made even greater than the old. The psalmist extols God's greatness and assures the people that God will save the faithful. The epistle calms the fears of early Christians who face a delay in the Lord's coming. As the firstfruits of salvation, sanctified by God's Spirit, we have nothing to fear. In Luke, Jesus confirms the truth of the resurrection, proclaiming that our God is God of the living, not the dead, and that those who rise again are like angels who can no longer die.

CALL TO WORSHIP (PSALM 145)
We extol you, our God and King.
Praise God's name forever and ever!
Great is the Lord, and greatly to be praised.
Praise God's name forever and ever!

The Lord is just and overflowing with kindness.
Praise God's name forever and ever!
The Lord is near to all who call.
Praise God's name forever and ever!
God saves us from our troubles.
Praise God's name forever and ever!
We extol you, our God and King.
Praise God's name forever and ever!

CALL TO WORSHIP (HAGGAI 1, 2 THESSALONIANS 2)

God's Spirit abides among us,
we have nothing to fear.
Though the earth shakes and the heavens tremble,
we have nothing to fear.
Though the seas roar and the land shudders,
we have nothing to fear.
God has chosen us as the firstfruits of salvation.
We are sanctified by God's Holy Spirit.
God's Spirit abides among us.
Come, let us worship.

CONTEMPORARY GATHERING WORDS (PSALM 145)

You are our King, O God.
We will praise your name forever!
Your greatness knows no bounds.
We will praise your name forever!
You watch over us, O God!
We will praise your name forever!
You never leave us at the mercy of our enemies.
We will praise your name forever!
You are our King, O God.
We will praise your name forever!

PRAISE SENTENCES (PSALM 145)

Extol our God, our Lord and King!
You are greatly to be praised!

Your glorious splendor is wondrous to behold.
You are greatly to be praised!
Extol our God, our Lord and King!
You are greatly to be praised!

OPENING PRAYER (HAGGAI 1)
Redeemer God,
   you make all things new.
When we look at our lives
   and see only devastation and loss,
   remind us that you are always with us.
Your Spirit abides within us.
We have nothing to fear.
Shake the heavens and earth once again,
   and fill our lives with your splendor.
Shake us from our complacency,
   and our defeatist attitudes,
   that we may see that the days ahead
      are filled with greater promise
         than the days we long to recapture. Amen.

OPENING PRAYER OR PRAYER OF CONFESSION (2 THESSALONIANS 2)
Living God,
   it is easy to become discouraged.
Our confidence is quickly shaken,
   our faith as fragile as a reed in a storm.
When we falter,
   remind us that we are your beloved children,
   sisters and brothers with Christ.
Teach us anew that you have chosen us
   as the firstfruits for salvation,
   through sanctification in the Spirit.
Comfort and strengthen us.
Give us the strength to stand firm and hold fast,
   that we may do every good work in your name.
Amen.

BENEDICTION (HAGGAI 1–2)
Take courage; God is with us.
God's Spirit abides among us.
Life is filled with the riches of God's blessings.
God's Spirit renews our lives.
With God, all things are possible.
God's Spirit makes us whole.

BENEDICTION (2 THESSALONIANS 2)
Now may the Lord Jesus Christ
bless us with comfort and hope.
May God, our guide and counselor,
comfort our hearts and strengthen us
in every good work and word.
Go forth in Christ's glory.
We go with God's blessings.

NOVEMBER 18, 2007

Twenty-fifth Sunday after Pentecost
John Brewer

COLOR
Green

SCRIPTURE READINGS
Isaiah 65:17-25; Isaiah 12; 2 Thessalonians 3:6-13; Luke 21:5-19

THEME IDEAS
The end is near. The end has always been, and will always be, near: the end of the year, the end of a season, the end of heaven and earth as we have known it. Along with the end comes a new beginning—a new heaven and a new earth. God will make this happen. In the meantime, we will be faced with transitions, difficulties, and even persecution for our beliefs. What we consider to be beautiful, God will "tear down." What we consider to be comfortable, God will disturb. New life comes through change. God, who never changes, has created a universe that is ever-changing. Yet God assures us that a new beginning is near. The new beginning is always near.

CALL TO WORSHIP (ISAIAH 65)
God will create a new heaven and a new earth.
**The former things will not be remembered,
nor will they come to mind.**

God rejoices over Jerusalem
and takes delight in all God's people.
The sound of weeping and crying
will be heard no more.
Before we call out, God will answer.
While we are still speaking, God will hear.
The wolf and the lamb will feed together,
and the lion will eat straw like the ox,
but dust will be the serpent's food.
They will neither harm nor destroy
on all God's holy mountain.
We worship the One who makes all things new!

CALL TO WORSHIP (ISAIAH 12)

We will praise you, O Lord.
Your anger has turned away,
and you have comforted us.
Surely God is our salvation.
We will trust and not be afraid.
The Lord is our strength and our song.
God has become our salvation.
With joy we draw water from the wells
of your salvation.
Give thanks to the Lord.
Call on God's name.
Make known what God has done.
We will sing to the Lord,
for God has done glorious things.

CONTEMPORARY GATHERING WORDS (LUKE 21)

We call ourselves Christians,
but we do not seem much like Christ, do we?
We call ourselves Christians,
but we do not like to suffer for it, do we?
The time will come when we will have to decide:
to stand firm in the Lord, or to slip away

into the ranks of uncommitted "believers."
Today, we gather to be noticed,
    not in a way that draws attention to ourselves,
    but in a way that draws attention to the living Christ.
We gather to be strengthened by Jesus,
    who goes with us into a world
      that sometimes hates us
      for being Christlike.
If we stand firm in our faith, we will gain life,
    through Jesus Christ, our Lord.

PRAISE SENTENCES (PSALM 146:1-2)

Praise the Lord, O my soul.
I will praise the Lord all my life.
I will sing praise to my God as long as I live.

PRAISE SENTENCES (PSALM 143:8)

Let the morning bring us word
    of your unfailing love, O God.
We have put our trust in you.
Show us the way we should go,
    for to you we lift up our souls.

PRAISE SENTENCES (PSALM 149:1-2)

Praise the Lord.
Sing to the Lord a new song.
Sing God's praises in the assembly of the saints.
Let the people be glad in their King.

OPENING PRAYER (LUKE 21)

O Lord of the universe,
    O God who never changes,
      be with us this day,
      as we gather in the face
        of an ever-changing world.
We seek your steadfast mercy

and your unconditional love.
We seek the guidance of your Holy Spirit,
   as we face competing demands for our loyalty.
We seek the salvation
   that comes through your Son, Jesus Christ.
May our comfort be in you alone, O God,
   through all the circumstances
     of our lives. Amen.

OPENING PRAYER (LUKE 21)

There is no place to turn, O God,
   for the comfort we desire;
   no place, but to you alone, O Lord.
Bless us this day,
   that we might be blessings to others.
Bless us this day,
   that we might be faithful witnesses
     to the life and suffering of Jesus Christ,
     our Lord and Redeemer.
In our songs and prayers,
   in our scriptures, spoken words, and hymns,
   reveal to us the purpose
     for which we have been called
       by your Holy Spirit.
Here we are, O Lord.
Equip us for ministry
   with the faith and assurance
     only you can provide. Amen.

PRAYER OF CONFESSION (LUKE 21)

In complete humility, O Lord,
   we bow before you this morning
     to acknowledge our sinfulness.
We ask forgiveness:
   for words spoken in cruelty;
   for behavior that tears down,

rather than building up;
for failure to take responsibility
for the ministries of your church;
for preferring temporal wealth
over being rich in spirit.
Forgive us, we pray,
and lead us into fullness of life,
through Jesus Christ our Lord. Amen.

BENEDICTION (2 THESSALONIANS 3)
May the strength of God be with you,
that you will never tire
of the work God calls you to do
for the benefit of God's kingdom on earth.
Go forth with the power of God's Spirit,
to share the life of the gospel
with all those you meet in the days ahead.
Christ is alive. Christ is alive in you! Amen.

BENEDICTION (LUKE 21)
Go forth and stand firm,
that you will gain life
in the presence of God,
who has created you,
and who sustains you,
through the challenges of each week.
Remember that in every circumstance,
you will be challenged
to change the world around you,
as you reflect the light of Christ.
Stand firm, and you will gain life
in the living God.

NOVEMBER 22, 2007

Thanksgiving Day
B. J. Beu

COLOR
Red or White

SCRIPTURE READINGS
Deuteronomy 26:1-11; Psalm 100; Philippians 4:4-9;
John 6:25-35

THEME IDEAS
God provides everything we need. In the face of God's
wonderful abundance, we are called to rejoice. To this
general call to rejoice and celebrate, Deuteronomy
adds the specific instruction to give back to God from
the firstfruits of our harvest. Thanksgiving is a time to
focus, not on what we have, but on what God has
given us.

CALL TO WORSHIP (PSALM 100)
Make a joyful noise to the Lord, all the earth!
Worship the Lord with gladness!
Come into God's presence with singing!
Enter God's gates with thanksgiving!
Give thanks to the Lord, for God is good!
God's steadfast love endures forever!

CONTEMPORARY GATHERING WORDS (PHILIPPIANS 4)

Rejoice in the Lord always!
Again I say rejoice!
Thank you, God,
for the homes we live in.
Rejoice in the Lord always!
Again I say rejoice!
Thank you, God,
for the food we have to eat.
Rejoice in the Lord always!
Again I say rejoice!
Thank you, God,
for the blessings you bring us.

PRAISE SENTENCES (PSALM 100, PHILIPPIANS 4)

Rejoice in God always.
Come into God's presence with thanksgiving.
We rejoice in our God!
Worship the One whose steadfast love
endures forever!
We rejoice in our God!
Worship God with gladness in your hearts!
We rejoice in our God!
Enter God's gates with songs of thanksgiving and praise.

OPENING PRAYER (DEUTERONOMY 26, JOHN 6)

Almighty God,
you have led us into a land
flowing with milk and honey.
As we rejoice in your manifold blessings,
help us remember those
who have no bread to eat.
As we celebrate the bounty of your table,
remind us to seek
the food that does not perish.

Help us listen to the words of your Son:
"I am the bread of life.
Whoever comes to me
 will never be hungry,
and whoever believes in me
 will never be thirsty." Amen.

OFFERTORY PRAYER (DEUTERONOMY 26, JOHN 6)

Bountiful God,
 you cause the earth
  to bring forth food
   for the harvest;
 you cause rain
  to kiss the ground
   and sustain our lives.
Receive these offerings,
 as the firstfruit of our labors.
May our offerings be acceptable to you,
 and go forth into the world
  as a sign of our joy and thankfulness.
In Jesus' name,
 who is the bread of life, amen.

BENEDICTION (PHILIPPIANS 4)

Hear the word of God:
 "Whatever is true, whatever is honorable,
 whatever is just, whatever is pure, whatever is pleasing,
 whatever is commendable, if there is any excellence
 and if there is anything worthy of praise,
 think about these things. Keep on doing the things
 that you have learned and received . . . ,
 and the God of peace will be with you."
Go with God's blessings.

BENEDICTION (PHILIPPIANS 4)

Do not worry about anything, but in everything you do,
let your requests be made known to God.

In prayer and supplication, with thanksgiving and shouts of joy, we will bring our lives before God. May the peace of God, which passes all understanding, guard your hearts and minds in Jesus Christ, our Lord. **Amen.**

NOVEMBER 25, 2007

Reign of Christ/Christ the King Sunday
Robert Blezard

COLOR
White

SCRIPTURE READINGS
Jeremiah 23:1-6; Luke 1:68-79; Colossians 1:11-20; Luke 23:33-43

THEME IDEAS
Redemption, protection, and God's love for humanity are themes woven throughout today's readings. But one theme is conspicuously absent—repentance for sin. Religious leaders are chastened today, and by extension people are cautioned to examine the leaders they follow. There is sin in the world, but today's scriptures blame the shepherds and kings, not their followers and subjects. Jeremiah scolds and warns the bad shepherds while foreseeing God's righteous king. Luke 1 recalls God's promise of deliverance—a promise being fulfilled in Christ. Colossians talks of rescuing us from the powers of darkness. Finally, Luke 23 provides the ultimate promise of deliverance and salvation, as Jesus utters blanket absolution for those responsible for his crucifixion.

CALL TO WORSHIP (JEREMIAH 23)
The hour has arrived.
We will follow Jesus.

Our shepherd and king has come.
We will follow Jesus.
A shepherd to rescue and protect us.
We will follow Jesus.
A king to rule with justice and wisdom.
We will follow Jesus.
The Lord is our righteousness.
We will follow Jesus.

CALL TO WORSHIP (LUKE 1)

Come into the light, all who sit in darkness
and in the shadow of death.
**Illuminate us, O God, and guide our feet
into the way of peace.**

CONTEMPORARY GATHERING WORDS (JEREMIAH 23)

Many of us here today have followed the wrong shepherd,
the wrong ruler. We have allowed ourselves to be ruled
by the allure of money, or fashion, or drugs, or alcohol,
or sex, or low self-esteem, or empty religiosity.
Save us, O God!
Come and hear the good news.
There is a new king in town and his name is Jesus.
He will protect you, and fight for you, and save you.
Thanks be to God!

PRAISE SENTENCES (COLOSSIANS 1)

A rescued people, we raise our voices to God!
We rejoice in the freedom of God's sovereignty!
Praise the One who has brought us out of darkness.
We rejoice in the light of God's sovereignty!

PRAISE SENTENCES (COLOSSIANS 1)

Sing praises to God, the Almighty!
God's love has set us free!

Sing praises to God, the Almighty!
God's light has brought us out of darkness!
Sing praises to God, the Almighty!
God's love has brought us here!
(B. J. Beu)

OPENING PRAYER (LUKE 1)

Holy God,
    by sending your Son, Jesus the Christ, into our world,
    you have ended our long night of darkness.
May your light always shine upon us—
    to nourish us, to guide us, and to teach us
        the ways we should go.
Be with us all,
    especially our young women and men.
Guide our schoolchildren,
    that as they learn their subjects,
    they might also learn your will
        and answer your call of discipleship. Amen.

OPENING PRAYER (COLOSSIANS 1)

God of mercy and love,
    you have rescued us from the power of darkness,
    and made us subjects of the benevolent reign
        of Jesus the Christ.
We are grateful for your presence among us now,
    as we worship you and open our hearts and souls
        to your holy Word.
Teach us, your disciples and your subjects,
    the ways of truth and love. Amen.

PRAYER OF CONFESSION (JEREMIAH 23)

O God, our shepherd and our sovereign,
    we have turned from you,
    and have listened to the calling
        of other shepherds—

shepherds who have left us scattered,
vulnerable, and afraid.
Forgive our foolishness, O God.
Help us hear and heed your merciful voice,
    calling to gather us, protect us, and give us life.
Amen.

WORDS OF ASSURANCE (LUKE 23 KJV)

Hear the words spoken by Jesus in his darkest hour:
"Forgive them, for they know not what they do."
In Jesus Christ, we are forgiven.

BENEDICTION (COLOSSIANS 1)

And now may the Almighty One,
    who is before all things, who created all things,
    and who reconciles all of creation in divine love,
    bless you and bring you peace through Jesus Christ.
Amen.

BENEDICTION (JEREMIAH 23)

From the corners of the world,
    God calls and gathers the flock.
May the Good Shepherd watch over you,
    dispel your fears, and bring you peace.

DECEMBER 2, 2007

First Sunday of Advent
Mary J. Scifres

COLOR
Purple or Blue

SCRIPTURE READINGS
Isaiah 2:1-5; Psalm 122; Romans 13:11-14; Matthew 24:36-44

THEME IDEAS
On this First Sunday of Advent, life and schedules are often filled with chaos and doubt. Today's scriptures recognize this reality in our world and in our lives. For thousands of years, God's people have been praying for peace. And yet, peace eludes us. For hundreds of years, we have been awaiting the return of Christ. And yet, we wait again this Advent season. We wait for peace. We wait for God. With hope and love, Advent calls us to wait.

CALL TO WORSHIP (ISAIAH 2, ROMANS 13)
We know what time it is—
the moment to wake from sleep.
We awaken to greet the day,
yearning for God's peace on this earth.
Let us lay down our swords
and put aside all works of darkness.

Let us walk in the light
and live as peacekeepers.
Let us worship our God
as expectant believers.
We worship with joy,
knowing Christ will come!

CALL TO WORSHIP (PSALM 122)

Were you glad when you heard God's call?
We were glad when Christ called us to love!
Will you come to the house of the Lord?
We have come to worship and praise our God!
Are your feet firmly planted here now?
We are standing on holy ground!
Let us pray for God's peace in our world.
We will seek God's goodness and love.

CALL TO WORSHIP (ISAIAH 2, PSALM 122)

Come to the house of the Lord!
Worship the God of Jacob!
Come to the mountain of God.
Pray for the word to shine clear.
Walk in the light of the Lord.
Walk in the pathways of peace.

CONTEMPORARY GATHERING WORDS (PSALM 122)

In this house of stone and light,
God is present.
In this place of worship and service,
Christ is living.
In this time of waiting and hoping,
the Spirit is calling:
"Come, let us go up to the house of the Lord."
We have come.
We are here.
Listen ...

Wait ...
Christ has come.
Christ is with us now.

Contemporary Gathering Words (Romans 13)

Wake up! The night is gone and morning has come!
Wake up and wait for the Lord!

Praise Sentences (Psalm 122)

Rejoice! We are in the house of the Lord!
Rejoice! Christ is coming soon!
Rejoice! Let us worship and praise!

Opening Prayer (Isaiah 2, Psalm 122)

We pray this day for peace:
peace for Jerusalem,
and the troubled land of her birth;
peace for your people,
scattered across this vast globe;
peace for your world,
groaning with injustice and war;
peace for our lives,
harried and troubled with strife.
Let your peace wash over us,
and shine out to your world.
Let your love overcome
the hatred that divides us.
As we move into this holy season of Advent,
may our lives be blessed with your peace—
the peace that passes all understanding.
And may your peace flow through us,
offering hope to a despairing world.
In hope and love, we pray. Amen.

Opening Prayer (Romans 13, Matthew 24)

Holy One,
we wait and hope for your peace.

We live in the promise of your love.
As the days darken and the nights lengthen,
   light our way with your promised presence.
Prepare us to celebrate your birth,
   and guide us to create your kingdom on earth.
In hopeful expectation we pray. Amen.

UNISON PRAYER (ROMANS 13)

Mighty God,
   strengthen us for the journey.
Clothe us with wisdom and grace,
   that we might walk in your light
   and shine your love
      into the darkest corners
      of this world.
Help us live as your people,
   honoring you in all that we say
   and all that we do.
And when the day of your return comes,
   welcome us as beloved children,
   that we might rejoice with the angels
   and sing with the saints. Amen.

PRAYER OF CONFESSION (ISAIAH 2, ROMANS 13)

God of grace and mercy,
   hear our confession:
      we have fashioned plowshares into swords,
         when we have chosen to fight,
         rather than seeking peaceful means
            to solve our conflicts;
      we have turned pruning hooks into swords,
         when we have offered criticism,
         rather than extending assistance.
Forgive us and grant us your grace.
Give us the patience to create peace
   in the midst of turmoil.

Give us the wisdom to offer love
where it is most needed.
Help us live as people
who are ready for your arrival
in our world. Amen.

WORDS OF ASSURANCE (ROMANS 13)
My friends, salvation is nearer to us now
than when we first became believers.
God is with us. Emmanuel.
God is with us now!

BENEDICTION (ISAIAH 2, PSALM 122)
Go in peace, for the God of peace goes before us.

BENEDICTION (PSALM 122)
Peace be with you, both now and forevermore.

BENEDICTION (ROMANS 13)
Let us live as children of light,
clothed in the love of Christ.
**Let us go forth, shining with hope
for all the world to see!**

DECEMBER 9, 2007

Second Sunday of Advent
B. J. Beu

COLOR
Purple or Blue

SCRIPTURE READINGS
Isaiah 11:1-10; Psalm 72:1-7, 18-19; Romans 15:4-13; Matthew 3:1-12

THEME IDEAS
Isaiah promises that a righteous branch shall grow out of the shoot of Jesse—a branch that will bring justice and peace, not only to the people, but to creation itself. Christians profess Jesus to be this branch, and we are called to get ready. Matthew warns us, however, that the peace promised by Isaiah will be accompanied by the destruction of the wicked. The axe is already lying at the root of the tree. It is time to lead lives worthy of repentance, in the name of the One who baptizes us with fire and the Holy Spirit. As Romans declares, the promises we have received in Scripture give us hope for the future.

CALL TO WORSHIP (ISAIAH 11)
A shoot has come forth from the stump of Jesse.
A holy branch has grown out of his roots.
The spirit of the Lord rests upon his shoulders—
the spirit of wisdom and understanding,

the spirit of counsel and might,
the spirit of knowledge and the fear of the Lord.
Righteousness is the belt around his waist.
And faithfulness is the mantle upon his shoulders.
Jesus stands as a signal to the peoples.
God's salvation is at hand.

CALL TO WORSHIP (MATTHEW 3)
Prepare the way of the Lord!
God's kingdom has drawn near.
Prepare the way of the Lord!
God's salvation is at hand.
Prepare the way of the Lord!
Christ the Lord is coming
with fire and the Holy Spirit.
Prepare the way of the Lord!
Blessed is the One who comes
in the name of the Lord.

CONTEMPORARY GATHERING WORDS (MATTHEW 3)
Pay attention, the kingdom of God draws near!
Prepare the way. The Lord is coming.
Get ready, the kingdom of God is at hand!
Prepare the way. The Lord comes
with the fire of the Holy Spirit.
Turn to God; Christ is on the way.
We are watching, waiting, and praying.
We are ready. Come, Lord Jesus, come.

CONTEMPORARY GATHERING WORDS (ISAIAH 11, MATTHEW 3)
Father Abraham is still with us.
Jesus is the promised child of God.
Hope is not lost.
Justice and mercy will be born anew.

Righteousness will win the day.
Repentance and forgiveness are at hand.
God's salvation has come near.
We are ready. Prepare the way of the Lord!

CONTEMPORARY GATHERING WORDS (ROMANS 15)

Rejoice in the Lord, all God's people!
Praise God's holy name!
Rejoice in the Lord, all God's people!
Praise God's holy name!
Let's praise the Lord!

CONTEMPORARY GATHERING WORDS OR PRAISE SENTENCES (PSALM 72)

Blessed be the Lord.
Bless God's glorious name forever!
Blessed be the Lord.
Bless God's glorious name forever!
Blessed be the Lord.
Bless God's glorious name forever!

PRAISE SENTENCES (ISAIAH 11)

God is great!
Sing glory to our God!
The Lord is mighty!
Shout praises to the Lord!
God is enthroned forever!
Praise God!

PRAISE SENTENCES (MATTHEW 3)

God's Spirit is upon us!
God's Spirit washes over us!
God's Spirit is upon us!
God's Spirit washes over us!

OPENING PRAYER (ISAIAH 11)

Prince of Peace,
in this season of Advent
we are reminded once again
that the spirit of the Lord
rests upon your shoulders:
the spirit of wisdom and understanding,
the spirit of counsel and might,
the spirit of knowledge and the fear of the Lord.
Be with us in our worship,
and lead us into your kingdom:
where the wolf lives with the lamb,
the leopard lies down with the kid,
and none shall hurt or destroy
on all your holy mountain. Amen.

OPENING PRAYER (MATTHEW 3)

Holy God,
we hear the words of John the Baptist anew:
"Repent, for the kingdom of heaven
has come near."
Help us bear fruit worthy of repentance,
that our lives may be transformed
by the power of our baptism in Christ—
a baptism of fire and the Holy Spirit.
Prepare our hearts
to receive your Son once more,
as we gather to worship you this morning. Amen.

BENEDICTION (ROMANS 15:5-6)

May the God of steadfast love and encouragement
grant you to live in harmony with one another,
in accordance with Christ Jesus,
so that together you may with one voice
glorify the God of our Lord Jesus Christ.

BENEDICTION (ROMANS 15:13)
May the God of hope
  fill you with all joy
  and peace in believing,
  that you may abound in hope
    by the power of the Holy Spirit.

DECEMBER 16, 2007

Third Sunday of Advent
Mary Petrina Boyd

COLOR
Purple or Blue

SCRIPTURE READINGS
Isaiah 35:1-10; Luke 1:47-55; James 5:7-10; Matthew 11:2-11

THEME IDEAS
A deep sense of joy pervades these readings, from the return of exile to Mary's song and Jesus' promise of healing and redemption. This joy is focused on those in need: those with limiting physical conditions, those who are powerless, and those in economic distress. The reading from James counsels patience as we await the coming of the Lord.

CALL TO WORSHIP (LUKE 1)
God our Savior looks with favor upon us.
My soul magnifies the Lord!
And my spirit rejoices in God my Savior.
God has done great things. Holy is God's name.
My soul magnifies the Lord!
And my spirit rejoices in God my Savior.
God brings down the proud, the powerful, and the rich.
My soul magnifies the Lord!

And my spirit rejoices in God my Savior.
God lifts up the lowly and fills the hungry
with good things.
My soul magnifies the Lord!
And my spirit rejoices in God my Savior.
God's mercy is from generation to generation.
My soul magnifies the Lord!
And my spirit rejoices in God my Savior.

CALL TO WORSHIP (ISAIAH 35)

The dry lands blossom.
Rejoice and give thanks.
Water flows in the desert.
God leads us to life.
God prepares a way for us.
We see God's glory.
Return to God with a song.
Sing with everlasting joy and gladness!

CALL TO WORSHIP (JAMES 5)

Christ is coming.
We wait for Jesus.
Be patient as you wait.
As the farmer anticipates the crop,
we anticipate Christ's coming.
Strengthen your hearts.
We prepare for the birth of love.
The coming of the Lord is near.
We wait with joy! Thanks be to God.

CONTEMPORARY GATHERING WORDS (ISAIAH 35)

Here is the highway, built by God.
We follow God's way.
Here is the holy way, built for God's people.
We go where God leads.
Come, walk in God's way.
We come with songs of joy!

PRAISE SENTENCES (JAMES 5)
The Lord is coming soon.
Be patient. Strengthen your hearts.
Jesus is coming!

PRAISE SENTENCES (LUKE 1)
God lifts up the lowly, and fills the empty with goodness.
We rejoice in our God, who saves us!
God's mercy is everlasting.
Thanks be to God!

PRAISE SENTENCES (ISAIAH 35)
Be strong; do not fear! Here is your God!
Rejoice and blossom. God is at work!
In the wilderness, God makes a new way.
God brings us hope.

OPENING PRAYER (ISAIAH 35)
Living God,
   in the deserts and the dry places of our lives,
      we struggle, powerless and weak.
Lead us to places of healing,
   where we may grow in the power of your love,
   where we may flourish in the waters of Life,
   and where we may find everlasting joy
      and gladness. Amen.

OPENING PRAYER (LUKE 1, MATTHEW 11)
Mighty One,
   you have blessed our lives.
You came in Jesus,
   bringing healing and hope,
   restoring health and wholeness,
   and leading us in paths of righteousness.
Lead us now into your presence,
   that we may hear your word
   and wait with patience for your glory. Amen.

UNISON PRAYER (LUKE 1)

God of all people,
   you offer a word of grace
      to all who suffer,
   and a word of hope
      to all who despair.
Fill our hearts with a sense of your justice,
   that we may oppose evil powers
   and work for equality among all people.
Inspire us to share what we have with the world,
   that none may hunger,
   that none may be in want.
Show us how to overcome oppression,
   and bring hope to the powerless.
Make us your obedient people. Amen.

UNISON PRAYER (MATTHEW 11)

Almighty God,
   we are physical people,
      with real bodies,
      with real pain,
      and with real limits.
As Jesus cared for those in physical pain,
   bringing healing and hope,
   we remember all who suffer:
      those who are ill,
      those recovering from surgery,
      those with physical limitations.
Send your healing power upon them,
   and surround them with your love,
   that they may be strengthened.
Heal all of our brokenness,
   physical, mental, and spiritual,
   that we may serve you with joy. Amen.

PRAYER OF CONFESSION (ISAIAH 35)

You call us to walk in your ways, O God,
   but we are reluctant to follow—

our hearts are fearful,
our bodies are weak,
we are uncertain and afraid.
Give us courage to step out.
Help us accept your healing love.
Lead us in paths of justice,
and teach us to sing your praises. Amen.

WORDS OF ASSURANCE

God's mercy is everlasting.
Sing praise to God!

BENEDICTION (MATTHEW 11)

Go and tell the world about Jesus:
The blind see.
The deaf hear.
The lame walk.
The sick are healed.
The poor have hope.
Jesus is here, transforming the world.
In Jesus we are blessed.

BENEDICTION (JAMES 5)

Be patient and wait,
the coming of the Lord is near.
Strengthen your hearts,
that God may enter in.
Prepare for Christ's birth
and be blessed.

BENEDICTION (ISAIAH 35)

Go forth with God's blessing.
Follow God's ways with hearts filled with joy.
Walk with God in peace and harmony.
Share your gladness with the world.

DECEMBER 23, 2007

Fourth Sunday of Advent
Joanne Carlson Brown

COLOR
Purple or Blue

SCRIPTURE READINGS
Isaiah 7:10-16; Psalm 80:1-7, 17-19; Romans 1:1-7; Matthew 1:18-25

THEME IDEAS
On the fourth Sunday of Advent, we hear the prophet foretell of Emmanuel, we see Joseph's dream of Emmanuel, we hear the psalmist's longing for a savior, and we hear Paul's affirmation of a savior. On this Sunday before Christmas, we speak of God with us—in yearning, in promise, in certainty. It is an "almost ... not yet ... ah, it's here" time. Can we be open to the surprise of wonder a child of promise brings us this year?

CALL TO WORSHIP (ISAIAH 7, MATTHEW 1)
We have been looking for a sign.
    Emmanuel—God with us.
We have been waiting for a savior.
    Emmanuel—God with us.
The time is near—can it be?
    Emmanuel—God with us.
Come let us worship the God of sign,
wonder, and promise.

CALL TO WORSHIP (ISAIAH 7, PSALM 80, ROMANS 1, MATTHEW 1)

The prophet foretold it, the psalmist longed for it,
Joseph dreamed of it, Paul proclaimed it.
God is come to us, to be with us, to restore us, to save us.
Let us come in awe and wonder,
to worship the God who makes it all so.

CONTEMPORARY GATHERING WORDS

Christmas is a time of anticipation.
We can hardly wait.
Christmas is a time of giving.
We are ready to receive.
Christmas is a time of hope and promise.
We are looking for it.
Could it be? Is it here? Let us come and see;
Let us open ourselves to the wonder of it all.

PRAISE SENTENCES (ISAIAH 7, PSALM 80, MATTHEW 1)

Stir up your might, O God,
and come to save us!
Emmanuel—God with us.
Restore us, O God.
Let your face shine,
that we may be saved.
Emmanuel—God with us.

OPENING PRAYER (ISAIAH 7, MATTHEW 1)

O God,
in this time of worship,
may we be open to your promises, your love,
and your transformation.
May we vision and dream.
May we be surprised.

May we receive the life you give us.
May we encounter Emmanuel—God with us.
And may we never be the same. Amen.

OPENING PRAYER (ISAIAH 7, MATTHEW 1)
We come this morning,
    tired from rushing around,
    tired of trying to meet
        the demands and expectations
        of the season.
Slow us down.
Help us center our thoughts.
Restore in us a childlike wonder,
    and a belief that dreams
        really do come true.
We call on your name.
Be with us and in us, Emmanuel.
Amen.

PRAYER OF CONFESSION
O God,
    we are easily distracted and slightly jaded,
        and cannot believe Christ is almost here.
There are still presents to be bought—
    never mind wrapped.
There are parties to attend, cookies to be baked,
    trees to be trimmed.
Sometimes we cannot wait
    until all this hubbub is over.
Where is the time to sit, to sleep—
    never mind to dream?
We can get so caught up in the busyness of the season
    that we miss the gift the season is meant to be.
We have heard the scriptures and stories so often
    that they have become white noise.
For our frenetic pace, for our exhaustion,

for our tunnel vision, for our missing the wonder
and awe of a baby born to fulfill promises
made long ago, forgive us.
Restore to us the sense of surprise
that you came to us as a little baby,
unexpected, yet longed for.
God of the visioners and dreamers,
may we always be ready
to receive your gifts. Amen.

WORDS OF ASSURANCE (ISAIAH 7, MATTHEW 1)
God comes to us in dreams and visions,
in prophecies and affirmations,
in longing and in hope,
in salvation through a little child.
Claim this promise for yourself,
and let God's healing love fill you.

BENEDICTION (ISAIAH 7, MATTHEW 1)
Look, a young woman is with child and shall bear a son.
He shall be called Emmanuel.
We go forth with anticipation and longing.
Share the good news—Emmanuel—God with us,
is coming.
**We go with joy and hope, trusting in the promises
of God.**

BENEDICTION (ISAIAH 7, MATTHEW 1)
Go forth with a dream in your soul
and a song in your heart,
knowing that God's promises
are always fulfilled.
The time is almost here.
Get ready for wonder!

DECEMBER 24, 2007

Christmas Eve
Bryan Schneider-Thomas

COLOR

White or Gold

SCRIPTURE READINGS

Isaiah 9:2-7; Psalm 96; Titus 2:11-14; Luke 2:1-20

THEME IDEAS

Christmas Eve is a night of joyful celebration, a night to shout and sing the coming of Jesus. This is not an empty celebration that should leave us exhausted, but rather a deeply filled celebration that looks beyond the actual birth of Christ. The reading from Titus reminds us that the celebration of Jesus' birth is just the beginning. The mystery of God with us is contained not only in birth, but also in suffering, death, and resurrection.

CALL TO WORSHIP (LUKE 2)

Augustus and Quirinius—
ancient names that seem odd to today's ears ...
characters in an ancient story
that we long to hear.
Nazareth and Bethlehem—
distant towns we know little about ...
places our hearts long for,
because of the One who traveled there.

We gather together to hear once more,
a story so ancient and yet so current,
so distant and yet so near.
We come to hear the story
of God coming to us.

CALL TO WORSHIP (PSALM 96)

Ascribe to the Lord honor and majesty.
Ascribe to the Lord glory and strength.
Ascribe to the Lord praise upon praise.
For God, the Lord, has come to us.
In flesh, the Mighty One dwells with us.

CONTEMPORARY GATHERING WORDS (ISAIAH 9)

Darkness—we who walk in darkness
have seen a great light:
a light that is a joy for all the earth,
a light that announces new life.
In joy we greet this light.
In this light we see that our savior has come.

CONTEMPORARY GATHERING WORDS (ISAIAH 9)

A child has been born for us,
whose name is called:
Wonderful Counselor—
Good Shepherd,
Deliverer,
Lamb of God,
The Word;
Mighty God—
First and Last,
Author of Life,
Morning Star,
The Light;
Everlasting Father—
Bread of Life,

Resurrection and Life,
Light of the World,
The Vine;
Prince of Peace—
　　Chief Cornerstone,
　　Lord of lords,
　　King of kings,
　　The Way.
He is Immanuel. God with us!

Praise Sentences (Isaiah 9, Luke 2)

God's salvation has come. Alleluia!
Christ is born.
Light has shined in our darkness.
Christ is born.
God's salvation has come. Alleluia!
(B. J. Beu)

Opening Prayer (Titus 2)

Grace of God,
　　you have brought salvation to all,
　　　　by the giving of yourself.
In your sacrifice of love,
　　you have redeemed us.
May we live lives that glorify you,
　　as we celebrate your birth
　　　　into this world. Amen.

Opening Prayer (Luke 2)

Holy God,
　　in days of old
　　you sent your angels
　　　　to tell shepherds the good news:
　　　　　　"To you is born this day a Savior,
　　　　　　the Messiah, the Lord."
Help us hear with the shepherds this good news,

that we too may glorify and praise you
for all that we have seen and heard. Amen.

CELEBRATION OF CHRIST'S BIRTH

*(The following could be used in conjunction with the Taizé
chant, "Jubilate Coeli," or other simple song of joy.)*
Heaven sings:
   sing of creation and life;
   sing of love and light.
Earth sings:
   join the chorus, tell the story of salvation.
Let all welcome the Messiah.
Sun and moon proclaim the message of divine light.
Ocean waves tell of life-giving water.
Forests rustle with Spirit-filled wind.
Field and vineyard give fruit for a heavenly feast.

All peoples marvel at what they see and hear.
Join with all of creation in praise.
Sing of God's deeds of power and grace.

For Jesus Christ is born this day:
   the One who was foretold by the prophets,
     and promised in ages past;
   the One who would triumph over death,
     and bring us life;
   the One who would forgive our sin,
     and heal our wounds;
   the One who would show us the kingdom of God,
     and how we might live.

Born to set us free ...
Born to give us life ...
Born as a gift ...

Heaven sings and earth rejoices:
   Jesus Christ is born.

BENEDICTION (ISAIAH 9, TITUS 2)

In darkness we arrived.
In light we now leave.
Though once we stumbled,
we now walk with confidence.
Rise up and go, for the grace of God has appeared,
bringing salvation to all.
May the light of Christ lead us forevermore.

BENEDICTION (PSALM 96, LUKE 2)

Go, singing a song to the God of our salvation.
Sing of mighty deeds and glory.
Join the heavenly chorus and sing:
"Glory to God in the highest heaven,
and on earth peace."
Sing of God's salvation from day to day.
Jesus Christ is born today!

DECEMBER 30, 2007

*First Sunday after
Christmas/Epiphany Sunday*

Mark Dowdy

COLOR
White

SCRIPTURE READINGS
Isaiah 63:7-9; Psalm 148; Hebrews 2:10-18; Matthew 2:13-23

THEME IDEAS
The psalmist puts it well: "Hallelujah! Praise God from the heavens, praise God in the heights! Praise God, all you angels; praise God, all you multitudes in heaven! . . . Young men and women alike, old and young together! Let them praise the name of God, for God's name alone is exalted" (Psalm 148:1-2, 12-13*a*, *The New Testament and Psalms, an Inclusive Version*). What better words to welcome the Prince of Peace, the Holy One of God? Praise for all creation! Praise for God come among us! Praise in the carols we sing throughout this Christmas season!

CALL TO WORSHIP (PSALM 148, GNT)
(As a variation, alternate men and women reading the congregational responses.)
Praise the Lord! Let all the angels praise the Lord.

263

Praise him, sun and moon;
praise him, shining stars;
praise him, highest heavens.
Let them all praise the name of the Lord!
God commanded, and the universe
was created, fixed in place forever.
Praise God,
Kings and all peoples, princes and all other rulers,
girls and young men, old people and children too.
Let us all praise the name of the Lord,
and worship the Prince of Peace.

CALL TO WORSHIP (PSALM 148)

Praise the Lord! Praise the Lord from the heavens!
Let the sun and the moon, and the stars in the sky,
sing praises to our God!
Praise the Lord! Praise the Lord from the earth!
Let the mountains and the hills, the fruit trees
and tall cedars, sing praises to our God!
Praise the Lord! Praise the Lord all you peoples!
Let the old and the young, the mighty
and the meek together, lift their voices
and praise God's holy name!
Praise the Lord!
(B. J. Beu)

CONTEMPORARY GATHERING WORDS
(ISAIAH 63, *THE MESSAGE*)

Make a list of God's gracious dealings,
all the things God has done that need praising:
The generous bounties of God,
and God's great goodness to all
the families of the earth!
Compassion lavished, love extravagant.
The most wondrous thing God ever did
was to come to us, to help us in person.

Out of God's own love and pity, God redeemed us.
God rescued us and carried us for a long time.
Let us worship and praise our Redeemer
this Christmastime!

PRAISE SENTENCES (PSALM 148)

Praise the Lord!
Praise God in the heavens!
Praise God in the mountains and seas!
Praise God in the sanctuary!
Let all the earth praise the name of the Lord!
Praise the Lord!
(B. J. Beu)

OPENING PRAYER (EPIPHANY, ISAIAH 60)

Christ, our Light and our Truth,
come into our lives,
and make us holy.
Come into this place,
and make it your sacred space.
Come into our world,
and make it your world—
a world of light and love.
As we lift our eyes to you,
let us behold your radiance.
As we proclaim your name
with praise and joy,
let us know your glory,
and your grace. Amen.
(Mary J. Scifres)

OPENING PRAYER (PSALM 148)

Holy Creator, loving God,
we thank you for the special gift
of your child Jesus.
Generous Creator, giving God,

with the moon and stars,
 and all that lives,
 we join in praise and thanks! Amen.

PRAYER OF CONFESSION (MATTHEW 2)
Like King Herod before us,
 we hunt down that which threatens our way of life,
 and we want to kill.
When we feel tricked by those who outsmart us,
 we fly into a rage and want to destroy
  that which threatens us.
Forgive us, O God.
Give us sight and insight
 to set aside our fragile egos,
 and to flee into your loving and protective arms,
 in the name of Jesus Christ, the Prince of Peace.
Amen.

ASSURANCE OF PARDON
As Mary and Joseph and Jesus settled in Nazareth,
 help us know that you also take up residence in us,
 to be birthed each day, and to forgive our threats,
 our rages, and our destructive desires.
In the name of Jesus, Prince of Peace, we are forgiven!

PRAYER OF CONFESSION (EPIPHANY, MATTHEW 2)
Light of the world,
 shine upon us.
Shine into the darkness
 of our hate and fear,
 that we may be a people
  of light and love.
Shine into the darkness
 of our cruelty and oppression,
 that we may be a people
  of justice and righteousness.

Shine into the darkness
of our ignorance and false beliefs,
that we may be a people
guided by your truth.
Light of the world,
shine upon us,
that we may reflect your light
for all the world to see! Amen.
(Mary J. Scifres)

BENEDICTION (HEBREWS 2, *THE MESSAGE*)

Let us go into the new year with Jesus,
common in origin with us.
We go into the new year with Jesus,
who treats us as family, as brothers and sisters.
Let us go, placing our trust in God, just as Jesus did.
We go as children of God, with Jesus by our side.
And all of God's Christmas people say together:
Amen!

BENEDICTION (EPIPHANY, NEW YEAR)

May the grace of God lead you forth.
May the light of Christ shine on your paths.
May the presence of the Holy Spirit fill your days.
And may love be your way in the new year!
(Mary J. Scifres)

CONTRIBUTORS

ERIK J. ALSGAARD, father of Zach and Sarah, is an ordained elder in the Detroit Conference currently serving as communications director for the Baltimore Annual Conference.

LAURA JAQUITH BARTLETT is a United Methodist music minister in Oregon, where she lives with her husband and two daughters, all of whom enjoy Scandinavian folk dancing.

ROBERT BLEZARD is a freelance writer and editor with the Evangelical Lutheran Church in America.

MARY PETRINA BOYD is pastor of Coupeville United Methodist Church on Whidbey Island, Washington. She spends alternate summers working as an archaeologist in Jordan.

THE REVEREND JOHN A. BREWER is pastor of Salmon Creek United Methodist Church in Vancouver, Washington, after serving eight years as a district superintendent.

JOANNE CARLSON BROWN has the joy of being both a local church pastor at United Church in University Place, Washington (a joint United Methodist—United Church of Christ congregation), and an adjunct professor in the

School of Theology and Ministry at Seattle University. She journeys through life with her wee westie, Thistle.

MARK DOWDY is pastor of The United Churches of Olympia, a Federation of the United Church of Christ and the Presbyterian Church (USA), in Olympia, Washington.

REBECCA GAUDINO is a UCC minister and writer, living in Portland, Oregon.

JAMIE GREENING is the senior pastor of First Baptist Church, Port Orchard, Washington.

BILL HOPPE is the music coordinator and keyboardist for Bear Creek United Methodist Church in Woodinville, Washington, and is also a friend of Aslan.

HANS HOLZNAGEL, a member of Archwood United Church of Christ in Cleveland, Ohio, has worked in news, public relations, mission interpretation, and administration for the national ministries of the United Church of Christ for more than twenty years.

SARA DUNNING LAMBERT is a child of God who is privileged to be a wife, mother, and nurse. She is also the worship coordinator at Bear Creek United Methodist Church in Woodinville, Washington.

BRYAN SCHNEIDER-THOMAS is pastor of Amble United Methodist Church in Michigan, and director of the Guild of Parish Artists.

MARY J. SCIFRES serves as a consultant in leadership, worship, and evangelism from her Gig Harbor home near Seattle, where she and her husband, B. J., reside with their young son, Michael. Her books include *The United Methodist Music and Worship Planner* and its ecumenical counterpart *Prepare!* and the worship evangelism book *Searching for Seekers*.

B. J. BEU is pastor of Fox Island United Church of Christ, near Gig Harbor, Washington. A graduate of Boston University and Pacific Lutheran University, Beu has chaired the worship committee for the Pacific Northwest Annual Conference of the United Church of Christ, and was a member of the worship planning team for the Fellowship of Methodists in Music and Worship Arts National Convocation in Dearborn, Michigan.

SCRIPTURE INDEX